Dancing
BEYOND
Thought

Bhagavad Gita Verses
and
Dialogues on Awakening

GARY WEBER PH.D.

ISBN: 1482543958
ISBN-13: 9781482543957

Library of Congress Control Number: 2013906793
CreateSpace Independent Publishing Platform
North Charleston, South Carolina

Praise for *Dancing Beyond Thought: Bhagavad Gita Verses and Dialogues for Awakening*

Layer by layer the self who "I" thought I was falls away in the sonic and semantic realm of the Gita. Rather, "I" see, chanting, that these aspects of my self that I held so dear, that I would fight for with all of my passion, were never there in the first place, like the top step in a long staircase that only my foot imagines to be there, and it comes down on nothing at all but the landing with a thud.

In the silence that ensues, there is space only for laughter. By distilling the seven hundred Gita verses down to this deeply resonant quintessence of sixty, Weber has remixed a potent brew into just the stuff for the infoquaked present in love with complexity, bent over its phone, wondering about everything but the present moment and the nature of self. He shows us the treasure beneath our feet, the awareness right where we are.

From the foreword by Richard Doyle, Author of *Darwin's Pharmacy, Wetwares,* and *On Beyond Living*

"I'm sure many people will find it a very valuable tool...it's a fascinating and very useful way to present the Bhagavad Gita"

Robert Wright, Author of *The Evolution of God, Nonzero, The Moral Animal* and *Three Scientists and Their Gods*

Praise for *Happiness Beyond Thought: A Practical Guide to Awakening*

"Husband, father, scientist, military officer, and senior executive in industry and academia, Gary Weber has led a full and successful worldly life. Throughout all of this, Gary has relentlessly pursued a path of practice and inquiry in order to understand life and achieve enlightenment. It is rare to find one who has reached this goal, and rarer still to find such a one who has been so immersed in worldly life.

With this book, Gary has successfully integrated his profound realization with traditional non-dualistic teachings, as well as insights from Zen Buddhism and modern brain research, into a practical path that uses Yoga's time-tested practices of asana, pranayama, chanting and meditation to illumine a path to enlightenment for the modern reader."

Gary Kraftsow, author of *Yoga for Wellness* and *Yoga for Transformation*

"Gary Weber offers a treasure chest of practices for the serious practitioner seeking liberation. On your own journey towards awakening, savor these simple, easy to follow practices culled from Weber's study with his primary teacher Ramana Maharshi, his on-going exploration of Zen meditation practice, and the life-enhancing results of his experiments on the laboratory floor of his yoga mat."

Amy Weintraub, author of *Yoga for Depression*

"I've had the wonderful privilege of experiencing Gary in action over many years both as friend and teacher. Gary is the rare gem who points directly to what we really are at the heart of our being—timeless Presence—ever-present Stillness that is always immediately available; yet which we fail to recognize because of our over-identification with the changing circumstances of our lives. Gary offers us a fresh view, based on his firsthand experience of the paradox of enlightenment: that while there is nothing we can ultimately do to awaken to our timeless Presence, there are exquisite perennial practices of 'non-doing' that prepare the ground and clear the way for awakening. Gary beckons us to awaken from our dream of separation and realize our timeless and non-separate oneness with everything. Few may take up his call, but no pointer is more needed than his to call for us to come home."

Richard Miller, PhD author of *Yoga Nidra:*
The Meditative Heart of Yoga

Dedicated to Ramana Maharshi who found me lost and wandering in a dark forest, taught me what inquiry, love, and surrender were and brought nobody home...

ACKNOWLEDGEMENTS

My deepest appreciation for the kindness of Sri V. S. Ramanan, President of Sri Ramanasramam (Ramana Maharshi's ashram in Tiruvannamalai, South India) for his permission to use Ramana's "The Song Celestial: Verses from the Bhagavad Gita" and photograph. "The Song Celestial" is the backbone of the Gita verse selection.

My deep gratitude for the many hours and years I have shared with so many wonderful teachers and fellow travelers. Although too numerous to mention, those who had particular impact were Toni Packer, Roshi Eido Shimano, J. Krishnamurti, Swami Rama, Amrit Desai, Adyashanti, Gangaji, Poonjaji, Swami Viditatmananda, Gary Kraftsow, Richard Miller and of course my Sat Guru, Ramana Maharshi. No words would ever be enough.

Deep gratitude to those folk with whom I had the joy of doing this work. They are the voice of the Universe asking itself questions to which it already knows the answers, yet it still finds delight in the mysterious beautiful dance.

Special thanks to Rich Doyle for his foreword, many comments, helpful suggestions and editorial efforts. His great enthusiasm for working with the Gita was a continuing inspiration. It would have been a far different book without his inputs.

Special thanks also to Prasant Radhakrishnan for his valuable editorial and design comments.

Any net profits from this book will be donated to children's charities in South India, particularly those for the handicapped.

FOREWORD

The Quintessence of Gita Eloquence: Silent Mind, Joyful Mind

Dancing Beyond Thought isn't really *about* anything. It's a
cookbook for your head that goes something like this:"Take one
miserably noisy noggin, fold in selected Gita chants as translated
and distilled by a no-nonsense, no agenda, 21st century dude of
few thoughts, chill. Repeat. Repeat again. Allow to echo through
your noggin as you go about the apparently important activities
and trials of your day. Repeat. Sample for doneness – is there
anybody there who samples or chants? If no, then enjoy and
manifest infinite portions of happiness and delight. If yes, shut up
and chant!"

Seriously: As the great Bhakti poet Kabir put it,

Whatever I say, nobody gets it.
It's too simple.

I'll admit that when I first approached Gary Weber about studying
with him, I was attracted by the sheer wonder and perceived difficulty
of Sanskrit. It was hard, with symbols that did not easily resolve into
my sense of an alphabet. I liked to follow and form the curves that
make up the letters. Even the errors are fun. It is elaborate, with rules
of sandhi and treatises of rhetoric that detail proper composition for
diverse occasions. I was enthralled with all of this, because I had a
hunch that this tradition would shed much light on the limitations of
the Greek and Roman traditions of rhetoric that have informed our
so called "Western" sense of language and its capacities. Here was a
tradition that uses language not just to persuade, but to awaken and
heal. I was approaching Sanskrit as a scholar, and I was not wrong.
It's just that before I get to any of that, I just need to shut up and chant.

And when I do so, something more than language happens. When I chant "aham", for example, which is just close enough to its rough English equivalent "I am" for me to be able to remember it, something goes awry in my usual understanding of myself. Just who and what IS this "aham"? And why have I not paused to wonder just who this name "I" refers to? "Aham" is like a throat clearing on the "I" itself, as if to say 'Ahem, excuse me, just who might YOU be?"

Once upon a time, I would do anything to avoid that question; I would even deny that it is a question at all. The response was obvious. So I – ahem - would continue on with the chanting. "aham aatmaa gudaakesha sarva bhuuta ashaya sthitaH."

अहं	आत्मा	गुड़ाकेश	सर्व	भूत	आशय	स्थितः
aham-	aatmaa	gudaakesha	sarva-	bhuuta-	ashaya-	sthitaH
I am	the Self	always present	all	beings	heart	resides

Always present, I seemed to be going in circles. Now granted, the line is Krishna's, Arjuna's trusty charioteer who turns out to be a God, but if He is allegedly always present, residing in the heart of all beings, I could hardly escape the implication that I was starting to get an inkling who this "I" was. Now in my humble experience inklings are like dreams – best respected by being left uninterpreted - so I shut up and chant. Layer by layer the self who "I" thought I was falls away in the sonic and semantic realm of the Gita. Rather, "I" see, chanting, that these aspects of my self that I held so dear, that I would fight for with all of my passion, were never there in the first place, like the top step in a long staircase that only my foot imagines to be there, and it comes down on nothing at all but the landing with a thud.

In the silence that ensues, there is space only for laughter. By distilling the seven hundred Gita verses down to this deeply resonant quintessence of sixty, Weber has remixed a potent brew into just the stuff for the infoquaked present in love with complexity, bent over its phone, wondering about everything but the present moment and the nature of self. He shows us the treasure beneath our feet, the awareness right where we are. If only we will shut up and chant.

Astonishingly enough, I found Gary by chance, right where I am. I teach at a Major State University, and I was systemically looking around for a faculty member or graduate student who could help teach me Sanskrit, but none seemed to be available. Months passed, and each time I found a promising lead, it seemed to vanish. One day, after a lovely lunch with yet another lovely person who could not or would not teach me Sanskrit, I was biking home, and I made out a figure walking down the street. In an instant I recalled that we had taught some students in common, and I hailed him, somehow knowing his name as it came out of my mouth in something approaching a chant. He turned around, beaming, as if he had been waiting since the composition of the Gita itself for this particular chanting of his name. We got to talking, and yes, he knew some Sanskrit. There were no worries, no need to search for my Sanskrit teacher. I had been searching everywhere, across the globe, and right here in Central PA: "aham aatmaa gudaakesha sarva bhuuta ashaya sthitaH," if only we will shut up and chant, right where we are.

Richard Doyle

Author, *Darwin's Pharmacy*, *Wetwares*, and *On Beyond Living*

mobiused.wordpress.com

TABLE OF CONTENTS

Why the Bhagavad Gita and
Why this selection of verses?

Quite simply, this book arose because the Gita was the only scripture, aside from Ramana Maharshi's *Upadesa Saram*, and Shankara's *Nirvana Shatakam,* that really dealt accurately with the approach that unfolded on my path and what i was experiencing after "the page turned". As those texts are covered extensively in my earlier book, Happiness Beyond Thought: A Practical Guide to Awakening, and the Gita was covered in less depth, this book attempts to remedy that.

Also, as i worked with different folk, it was apparent that some "authoritative" text was necessary to cite to convince folk that i was not "making this up"; there was history and precedent behind the work. These approaches and experiences are generally unfamiliar to Westerners, and are not well described, if at all, in the main Christian and Tibetan and Theravadan Buddhist teachings.

The Bhagavad Gita was probably written about 2500 years ago. It is taken as part of the Upanishads, probably added after the first original texts, and is generally accepted with the same regard as those texts, as "shruti" or "revealed texts", literally "heard texts", i.e. the word of God, or as the title literally translates, The Song of God, by the Hindus, and increasingly by others as well.

It has been an important text for millennia in the Asian subcontinent, as well as China and Japan and ultimately world-wide.

The Gita has been translated into virtually every language and there are over 100 different translations in English. Many Westerners, including Robert Oppenheimer, Aldous Huxley, Henry David Thoreau (who had the largest collection of Sanskrit writings in America in his time), Ralph Waldo Emerson, Mahatma Gandhi, and Schopenhauer were serious readers of the Gita. It forms the basis of two of the chief works of Mahayana Buddhism, the Mahayana-sraddhotpatti and the Saddharma-pundariika. It is widely regarded as one of the greatest books of any time.

The Gita takes place on a battlefield as a discussion between Krishna, the incarnation or embodiment of God, and Arjuna, a famous warrior, who is heavily conflicted, and as the introductory verse states, with his eyes full of tears, agitated, despondent and pitiful. Should he fight or not, as he has relatives on both sides of the battle? This is a thinly veiled metaphor as the Gita is really about the "battle" of everyday life, for everyone, and the choices and conflicts they face in trying to find a way to function effectively, peacefully and sanely, perhaps to develop "self mastery".

Arjuna, throughout the Gita, is asking Krishna how he should live his life, how he can get rid of his sorrow and pain, and how he can be at peace and function effectively in his complex world. Arjuna will be called many different names throughout the Gita, probably for literary effect and emphasis, relating to his prowess as a warrior, his family lineages (son of Kunti, Bharata), etc.

References to Arjuna, by any of the many names used for him in the Gita, have not been used in the translations, as often they are for matching meters in given lines, and are confusing unless one knows how each of those names is derived. It was also used for emphasis and to indicate who was speaking; since this selection only uses verses that Krishna has spoken, that is unnecessary.

"Sanjaya", the ostensible author of the Gita is translated as "scribe", or "writer". It is not clear if the Gita was written by one, or several, folk, or if it was all written at the same time. It has been passed down orally through millennia, even before the written word, and has been, and still is, chanted in its entirety in its original version in Sanskrit.

Sanskrit, because of its "scientifically" logical construction, carefully prescribed grammar and phonics, and not having been used as a "working language", like English or French, is virtually unchanged over that time frame. Not being used as a "working" language, it was not subjected to the vagaries of daily use and modification by incorporating pieces and parts of other languages, or by creating new technologically-useful words, like googleing, texting, or skyping, much like Latin as compared to Italian.

The current text is drawn from several sources which the author has found useful, including "The Song Celestial; Verses from the Bhagavad Gita" by Ramana Maharshi, "The Bhagavad Gita" by Swami Sivananda, "Bhagavad Gita With the Commentary of Shankaracharya" by Swami Gambhirananda, "The Aruna Sanskrit Language Course: Unlock the Bhagavad Gita in its Sacred Tongue" by A. K. Aruna, "Bhagavad Gita Home Study Program by Swami Dayananda Saraswati", "The Bhagavad Gita: A Selection" by Ramesh Balsekar and the Bhagavad Gita Sanskrit course at the American Sanskrit Institute by Vyaas Houston. These texts range from as long as 1800 pages and 5 volumes to a mere 31 pages; length is no measure of impact or "value" as each has its own purpose.

It is said by many spiritual masters that one can take virtually any verse in the Gita and make that your long-term meditation practice. Entire spiritual disciplines and teachings arose, and lives were dramatically changed from just one verse. The famous teacher, Swami Vivikenanda, had his entire life changed by Chapter 2, Verse 3; "O, Paartha, yield not to unmanliness. This does not benefit you. O scorcher of foes, arise, giving up the petty weakness of the heart." After hearing it, he embarked on his great efforts to bring Hinduism to the entire Western world including his famous speech at the Parliament of the World's Religions in Chicago in 1893.

The Gita is great literature, as well as great poetry, and a wonderfully constructed, timelessly useful, "psychological" text on the human condition. It is amazing that our species has changed so little psychologically in 2500 years despite the astonishing changes in technology, communication, education, science, physics, etc.

This text is to be used, worked with, and understood, not as a "must do" requirement, but as a fascinating discovery and exploration of the layers upon layers of understandings and meanings contained in many of these beautiful and poetic verses, particularly when they are learned and chanted in Sanskrit.

Many of the metaphors are insightful and powerful, and like all great poetry, have a message behind/under the words, that continues to unfold its timeless mystery as one dances with them. i have spent countless priceless hours, learning, chanting, and being absorbed in "The Song Celestial", Ramana Maharshi's selection of verses.

The verses that are selected, 60 out of the 700 verses in the Gita, are those that the writer has found particularly useful for "awakening", and especially for "nondual", or "Advaitic" practices. The verses from "The Song Celestial" are the core of the selection; others arose from other sources as they danced.

Some "good" and "famous" verses are not here; they were not as useful in my practices and working with others. The selection was made to include fewer, really useful verses, for focus, pondering, and absorption, and to fully capture the essence of the Gita in an easily accessible form. If one wants the complete 700 verses, there are many other excellent books.

In my experience, chanting the Gita is a powerful and transformative process. This number of verses, about 60, is what i have found is chantable in about 40 minutes if one wants to retain any sense of what is being chanted and allow the chants to deepen, be absorbed and work their magic. If you chant them daily, even if you chant only half of them and the other half the next day, you will find them shifting with new meanings being intuited most days in some verses.

To avoid needless confusion, the term "Self" will be used for "the Universe", "Universal Consciousness", "Oneness", "Atman", Brahman", "Presence", etc. This is the approach that was used by the 8th century ACE codifier of Advaita Vedanta, Adi Shankara. These different terms arose from different folks' attempts to somehow describe the transcendent and ineffable. There are some nuances that some philosophers will quibble over which do not concern us here.

There are some complex rules in Sanskrit called "sandhi" governing how sounds are joined across word boundaries and how that changes due to neighboring sounds or the grammatical function of adjacent words.   i've chosen to not engage sandhi, and to use individual words rather than combined ones wherever possible for the transliteration and translation as the focus is on understanding. If one does chant this "non-sandhi" version, it is easy to feel the "sandhi-ed" version emerging naturally.

Often "I" is replaced by an "i", but not consistently, on purpose. This can be a useful reminder that the "I" is only a construct and, as our cognitive neuroscience has shown us, really doesn't exist as an "entity", only an ad-hoc functionality.

The Sanskrit is that generated by the Google transliteration tool which is available to anyone. It is easy to use yourself, easy to read and does not have some of the artistic flourishes found in some Sanskrit fonts that can make for difficult deconstruction and confusion.

The transliterated Sanskrit, which gives English representations of the Sanskrit sounds, has also been simplified. Palatal (P) and cerebral (C) sibilants are both "sh". No distinction is made

5

between the guttural, P, C and dental (D) "n"s. No distinction is made between the C and D aspirated or unaspirated, "t"s or "d"s. Anusvaara (nasalized preceding vowel) is indicated by an "M" and visarga (aspirated preceding vowel) by an "H".

In chanting the text, if you see a capital M or H, then make the preceding vowel sound more into your nasal cavity as an "m" for the M, and like a "haaha" with more aspiration for the H. Sanskrit "a" sounds like the "o" in "son" or like "ah"; "c" like the "ch" in "chunk". Pronounce the Sanskrit "t", "d" and "n" with the tongue against the back of the teeth, making a slight "thah", "dhah" and "nhah". If you see a "t, d, or n" with an "h" after it, like "th", that is a further aspirated version like "thhah" like the "th" in an*t*-*h*ill Pronounce "i" like in "if"; "e" like the "a" in "play"; "u" like in "full". Double consonants like "aa" are twice as long with more aspiration, like "aah".

This is not perfect Sanskrit, but it will be about 92.36% correct, more or less. In my experience, it captures much of the power of the Sanskrit without moving past the point where many Western students are put off by it. Listening to someone else chant it is very helpful. All of the verses are chanted, in order, in a video on YouTube (Gary Weber – Bhagavad Gita).

WHAT IS THE "PURPOSE" OF THE BHAGAVAD GITA?

II, 1

सञ्जय उवाचा
Sanjaya uvaaca

Sanjaya said

तं	तथा	कृपया	आविष्टं	अश्रु	पूर्ण	आकुल	ईक्शनम्
tam	*tathaa*	*kripayaa*	*aavishtam*	*ashru*	*puurna*	*aakula*	*iikshanam*
to him	thus	by pity	overwhelmed	tears	full	eyes	troubled

विशीदन्तम्	इदं	वाक्यं	उवाच	मधुसूदनः
vishiidantam	*idam*	*vaakyam*	*uvaaca*	*madhusuudanaH*
who was sad	this	sentence	said	the destroyer of demons

To he who was overcome with pity and who was despondent, his troubled eyes filled with tears, Krishna, the slayer of Madhu, spoke.

WHAT IS MY RELATIONSHIP TO THIS BODY/MIND, AND WHAT IS THE SELF'S RELATION TO ME?

श्रि	भगवान		उवाचा
shrii	bhagavaan		uvaaca
Sri	Bhagavan (Krishna)		said

XIII, 1, 2

इदं	शरीरं	कौन्तेय	क्षेत्रं	इति	अभिधीयते
idaM	shariraM	kaunteya	kshetram	iti	abhidhiiyate
this	body	son of Kunti	field	thus	is called

एताः	यो	वेत्ति	तं	प्राहुः	क्षेत्रज्ञ	इति	तद	विदः
etad	yo	vetti	taM	praahuH	kshetrajna	iti	tad	vidaH
this	who	knows	him	call	knower of the field	thus	that	knower of

This body is known as the field; he who knows it is called the knower of the field by the wise.

क्षेत्रज्ञं	चा	अपि	मम	विद्धि	सर्व	क्षेत्रेषु	भारत
kshetrajnaM	ca	api	mam	viddhi	sarva	kshetreshu	bhaarata
knower of field	and	also	Me	know	all	in the fields	Bhaarata

क्षेत्र	क्षेत्रज्ञयोः	ज्ञानं	यत्	तद	ज्नामं	मतं	मम
kshetra	kshetrajnayoH	jnaanaM	yat	tad	jnaanaM	matam	mama
field	knower of the field	knowledge	which	that	knowledge	considered	my

And know that I am the knower of the field in all the fields. The knowledge of both the field and the knower of the field is considered to be the true knowledge.

The Self has knowledge of, and is, all of the body-minds, and all of the apparent different individuals who know those body-minds.

The body-mind (and its sensations, emotions and thoughts) is called the "field" because that is where the fruits of actions in the form of pleasure and pain manifest, grow, and are "harvested". Whoever knows this body-mind as an object and understands it as distinct from himself, the subject/witness/observer, understands the situation in a deeper and surprisingly different way.

If one can objectify something, anything, (s)he cannot be that object. This is one of the fundamental principles of non-dualistic understanding and opens the door to the entire wondrous approach of "not this, not this" or "neti, neti", which allows one to ultimately perceive directly "what this is".

9

WHERE IS THIS SELF?
WHAT DOES IT DO?

X, 20

अहं	आत्मा	गुडाकेश	सर्व	भूत	आशय	स्थितः
aham-	aatmaa	gudaakesha	sarva-	bhuuta-	ashaya-	sthitaH
I am	the Self	always present	all	beings	heart	resides

अहं	आदिश	चा	मध्यं	चा	भूतानाम्	अन्त	एव	चा
aham	adish	ca	madhyaM	ca	bhuutaanaam	anta	eva	ca
I am	creator	and	sustainer	and	all beings	dissolver	even	and

I am the Self dwelling in the Hearts of all beings.
I am the creator, sustainer and dissolver of all beings.

The second line can also be interpreted as "I am the beginning, the middle and the end of all beings"

The Self is in the hearts of everyone. It is the birth, the life, and the death of everyone. This is one of the most cited and powerful of the verses in the Bhagavad Gita. Two Indian sages of the 20th century, Ramana Maharshi and Ramesh Balsekar, said that this verse alone could be chosen as the sole focus of meditation to reach awakening.

This focus is not just on a casual reading and an "Oh, yeah, I got that". Really becoming absorbed in this verse, and allowing the understanding of the full meaning and implications to sink into your consciousness over time creates a profoundly different paradigm and world view.

Working with a verse like this can be done by repeating it first thing in the morning and last thing at night, or at periodic occasions during the day, silently to yourself before you eat, or drink a cup of coffee or tea. It only takes a few seconds, but you will find that the impact can be profound.

I AM WORRIED ABOUT DYING, WHAT HAPPENS WHEN I DIE?

II, 27

जातस्य	हि	ध्रुवो	म्र्त्युः	ध्रुवं	जन्म	मर्तस्य	च
jaatasya	hi	dhruvo	mrtyuH	dhruvam	janma	mrtasya	ca
those born	for	certain	death	certain	birth	those dead	and

तस्मात्	अपरिहार्ये	अर्थे	न	त्वं	शोचितुम	अर्हसि
tasmaat	aparihaarye	arthe	na	tvam	shocitum	arhasi
therefore	over an inevitable	fact	not	you	to grieve	ought

Whoever is born, for him, death is certain, and whoever dies, for him, birth is certain.

Therefore there is really no point in having anxiety or grieving over what is inevitable.

The classical reincarnation interpretation is that "you" as an individual entity will be reborn carrying over the fruits of your actions from life to life. While this is a widely-held religious belief, there are many scientific and pragmatic issues regarding exactly what it is that is carried over, and how, when, and by whom, it would be decided are its specific "good deeds" and "bad deeds".

It is impossible for us to know all of the sources of all of the elements of any current action. It is equally impossible to know all of the impacts and results that will occur to countless others as even one seemingly "unimportant" action dances forward through space-time bumping into and interacting with other beings and their actions.

What may look like a small "bad" thing this morning to "me", may result, in interacting with others, and their actions at some point in the future, in a large "good", or "bad" thing happening to another, or not.

An alternative interpretation to the classical view of reincarnation, which i find much more likely, and surprisingly comforting, is that as we realize that the "I"/ego is just an ad-hoc construct with no fundamental reality, it subsequently weakens and deconstructs. What would it be that would be reborn?

In my experience, there is really no one here that wants, needs, or that would be "worth" continuing as it is. Whatever residue there is, seemingly just dissolves into the sea of Self when death of the physical body-mind occurs, to be used as some element of some future entity, or entities, or not, as the Self dances.

Whatever learning has occurred in and of the Dance, has already been integrated into the vast Self and is available universally to all beings now and in the future. It can also be looked at as having affected the memes of the existent beings in whatever way it manifested, so no continuation is necessary.

WHAT ARE THE CHARACTERISTICS AND NATURE OF THE SELF?

II, 20

न	जायते	म्रियते	वा	कदाचित्	न	अयं	भूत्वा	अभविता
na	jaayate	mriyatae	vaa	kadaacit	na	ayaM	bhuutvaa	abhavitaa
not	born	dies	and	at any time	not	Self	having been	cease to be

व	न	भूयः
vaa	na	bhuuyaH
and	not	again

अजः	नित्यः	शाश्वतः	अयं	पुराणः	न	हन्यते	हन्यमाने
ajaH	nityaH	shashvataH	ayaM	puraanaH	na	hanyate	hanyamaane
unborn	eternal	undecaying	Self	ancient	not	is destroyed	is destroyed

शरीरे
shariire
body

Self is not born, nor does Self ever die, nor having been, does Self ever cease to be. Self is birthless, eternal, undecaying, ancient; Self is not destroyed when the body is destroyed.

II, 24

अच्छेद्यः	अयं	अदाह्यः	अयं	अक्लेद्यः	अशोष्यः
acchedyaH	ayam	adaahyaH	ayam	akledyaH	ashoshyaH
cannot be cut	Self	cannot burn	Self	cannot be wetted	cannot be dried

एव	चा
eva	ca
also	and

नित्यः	सर्व	गतः	स्थाणुः	अचालः	अयं	सनातनः
nityaH	sarva	gataH	sthaanuH	acalaH	ayaM	sanaatanaH
eternal	all	pervading	immovable	unmoving	Self	changeless

The Self cannot be cut, burnt, wetted or dried. It is eternal, all pervading, immovable, unmoving, and changeless.

II, 17

अविनाशि	तु	तत्	विद्धि	येन	सर्वं	इदं	ततं
avinaashi	tu	tat	viddhi	yena	sarvam	idam	tatam
indestructible	but	Self	know	by which	all	this	is pervaded

विनाहं	अव्ययस्य		अस्य	न	कश्चित्	कर्तुम्	अर्हति
vinaasham	avyayasya		asya	na	kashcit	kartum	arhati
destruction	which does not change		Self	not	anyone	to do	is able

Know that the Self which pervades all this is indestructible. No one is able to destroy the Self, which does not change.

II, 16

न	असतः	विद्यते	भावः	न	अभावः	विद्यते	सतः
na	asataH	vidyate	bhaavaH	na-	abhaavaH	vidyate	sataH
no	the unreal	has	being	no	non-being	has	Self

उभयोः	अपि	द्रष्टः	अन्तः	तु	अनयोः	तत्त्व	दर्शिभिः
ubhayoH	api	drshtaH	antaH	tu	anayoH	tattva	darshibhiH
both	also	is realized	conclusion	indeed	of these	of truth	by seers

The unreal has no being, the Self has no non-being. Indeed, both of these conclusions have been realized by the seers of truth.

The phenomenal world of names and forms is ever changing, and is hence defined as "unreal" in a material sense. The changeless Self always exists. It can be known and seen directly, moment by moment, that this world is like a dream. The world appears like a mirage mistaken for water in the desert; it still remains but is known to be unreal.

The Self, then, has a host of attributes; it always exists, it pervades everything, is indestructible, cannot be cut or burned, cannot even be wetted or dried. It is immovable, unmoving and unchanging. Even when the body dies, it continues to exist.

These attributes are not mere spiritual hyperbole; they can serve as useful tools to look for the Self, and "see for your-self" if there might be such "stuff".

If one looks into a fire and sees something burning with all of the material forms changing, watch for what it is that isn't burned, that doesn't change. You see so many things changing in your life including your body-mind; look for what it is that doesn't change. Feel what it could be that would be all pervasive, not moving, and yet invisible and untouched by whatever happened to the forms it penetrates.

How does the Self not get affected By what the body-mind experiences?

XIII, 32

यथा	सर्व	गतं	सौक्ष्म्यात्	आकाशं	न	उपलिप्यते
yathaa	sarva	gatam	saukshmyaat	aakaasham	na	upalipyate
just as	all	pervading	being subtle	space	not	contaminated

सर्वत्र	अवस्थितः	देहे	तथा	आत्मा	न	उपलिप्यते
sarvatra	avasthitaH	dehe	tathaa	aatmaa	na	upalipyate
everywhere	present	in the body	so too	the Self	not	contaminated

Just as the all pervading space, being subtle is not contaminated, so too, the Self, present everywhere in the body is not contaminated.

What could this strange stuff be that exists everywhere, pervading everything and yet is unaffected by fire, explosions, destruction of the body-mind, hate, anger, fear, craving, love, pride, etc.? Could there be such a thing?

Perhaps a model is provided by what is called, in contemporary physics, Dark Energy, or now, the Higgs field. While is it strange and not fully understood, it does pervade every molecule, atom, and subatomic particle, every tooth, toenail, and hair. We do not know if it is self-conscious. As it permeates everything, including

18

us, we cannot "stand outside" and clearly observe it. It is likely that if it is self-conscious, it possesses an intelligence beyond ours. It may be that we are a way, a vehicle, through which it becomes self-conscious.

If we take our best scientific tools, and look as deeply as we can, we find we are nothing but patterns of waves of energy. There are validated quantum mechanical theories that explain how all matter is created from the Higgs field's interactions with certain waves of energy corresponding to "potential particles". Is this the Self of the Vedas?

IF I AWAKEN TO THE SELF, WILL I STAY THERE OR WILL I RETURN?

XV, 6

न	तत्	भासयते	सुर्यः	न	शशाङ्कः	न	पावकः
na	tat	bhaasayate	suuryaH	na	shashaankaH	na	paavakaH
not	it	illuminate	sun	not	moon	not	fire

यत्	गत्वा	न	निवर्तन्ते	तत्	धाम	परमं	मम
yat	gatvaa	na	nivartante	tat	dhaama	paramam	mama
which	reaching	do not	return	that	abode	supreme	is My

Neither sun, nor moon, nor fire illuminates the Self. Self is the supreme abode, reaching which, they do not return.

This popular verse appears as well in several Upanishads, including the Kathopanishad, Svetasvatara Upanishad and Mundaka Upanishad. Kathopanishad Ch. II, 5.15; "The sun does not shine there, nor do the moon and the stars, nor does this lightning shine and much less this fire. When Self shines, everything shines by Its energy, because It alone is self-luminous." Self remains even without the light of the sun, moon and fire.

20

VIII, 21

अव्यक्तः	अक्षर	इति	उक्तः	तं	आहुः	परमां	गतिं
avyaktaH	akshara	iti	uktaH	tam	aahuH	paramaam	gatim
unmanifest	immutable	thus	call	Self	they say	supreme	goal

यं	प्राप्य	न	निवर्तन्ते	तत्	धाम	परमं	मम
yam	praapya	na	nivartante	tat	dhaama	paramam	mama
which	gaining	not	return	that	abode	supreme	of mine

They say that the Self, which is unmanifest and immutable, is the supreme goal. That is the supreme abode. Those who reach it do not return to the world of illusion.

"Unmanifest" means that it cannot be directly perceived by the senses; it exists but there is no way that it can be detected, no way to know directly by seeing, hearing or smelling, that it is here and there and everywhere. "Immutable" means that it cannot be changed.

If one experiences that state, even briefly, they do not ever again fully believe that the world of illusion is real, substantial, concrete and "all there is". Once you have seen that there is a "black swan", there is never a return to the belief that all swans are white. If you see, from a high flying plane, or satellite picture, that the earth is curved, you will never again believe that the earth is flat or that you will fall off the edge.

Once you touch, directly, that great unchanging Self, you will never again believe that it doesn't exist, that there is not something that doesn't change, or that is beyond this world of the senses. It is so different from a white swan, that no one can ever convince you again that all swans are white.

You may then find yourself, beyond all reason, as i did, on a great quest to see (and be one with) the Self. If it dances that way, which is ultimately beyond your control, your efforts, persistence and surrender may have you abiding in that state, dissolving into the Self.

TO REACH THE SELF, WHAT WOULD I NEED TO WORK ON?

XV, 5

निर	मान	मोहा	जित	सङ्ग	दोषाः
nir	maana	mohaa	jita	sanga	doshaaH
free from	pride	non-discrimination	conquered	attachment	error of

Free from pride, lack of discrimination, those who have conquered the error of attachment

अध्य	आत्म	नित्या	वि	नि	वर्त्त	कामाः
adhya	aatma	nityaa	vi-	ni-	vrtta	kaamaaH
focused on	Self	always	completely	having	turned away from	desires

Focused always on the Self, having completely turned away from desires,

द्वन्द्वैः	विमुक्ताः	सुख	दुःख	संज्ञैः
dvandvaiH	vimuktaaH	sukha	duhkha	sanjnaiH
from dualities	freed from	pleasure	suffering	called

Freed from the dualities called pleasure and suffering

गच्छन्ति	अमूधाः	पदं	अव्ययं	तत्
gacchanti	*amuudhaaH*	*padam*	*avyayam*	*tat*
reach	the undeluded	state	undecaying	Self

The undeluded reach the undecaying, eternal Self.

WHAT IF I IGNORED WHAT I'VE READ OR STUDIED IN THE TEACHINGS?

XVI, 23

यः	शास्त्र	विधिं	उत्सृज्य	वर्तते	काम	कारतः
yah	shaastra	vidhim	utsrjya	vartate	kaama	kaarataH
one who	scriptures	injunctions	ignores	acts	by desire	as impelled

न सः	सिद्धिम्	अवाप्नोति न	सुखं	न	परां	गतिम्
na saH	siddhim	avaapnoti na	sukham	na	paraam	gatim
not he	success/maturity	gains not	happiness	not	supreme	state

He who abandons the injunctions of the scriptures and behaves as impelled by his desires, does not attain understanding for liberation, nor happiness, or the highest state, the Self.

The question often arises "But if i have no free will, what choice do i have in following the scriptures and in my behaviors?" That is absolutely correct; you ultimately have no free will, or choice. Whether or not you "awaken" is out of your hands, just as is your level of interest, dedication, faith, persistence, energy and ability to understand what arises. If you have "enough" of these, and if you know that you "must" awaken no matter what, you will – you will not fail.

25

What do i look for in order to see the Self?

XIII, 27

समं	सर्वेषु	भुउतेषु	तिष्ठन्तं	परमेश्वरम्
samam	sarveshu	bhuuteshu	tishthantam	parameshvaram
equally	in all	beings	residing	the Self

विनश्यत्सु	अविनश्यन्तं	यः	पश्यति	सः	पश्यति
vinashyatsu	avinashyantam	yaH	pashyati	saH	pashyati
among the perishable	the imperishable	one	who sees	he	sees

He who sees the Self, residing equally in all beings – the imperishable among the perishable – sees clearly.

This is one of the fundamental definitions of the Self, and how to hunt for it. In the course of your day, just keep looking for anything that does not change. Whether it's mountains, oceans, rocks, trees, folk, plants, animals, earth, emotions, desires, fears, sensations, etc., just keep seeing and inquiring, "Does this change?" Something, something, doesn't change, really...find it.

Is it possible to know or see the Self?

XI, 54

भक्त्या	तु	अनन्यया	शक्यः	अहम्	एवं	विधः	अर्जुन
bhaktyaa	tu	ananyayaa	shakyaH	aham	evam	vidhaH	Arjuna
by devotion	but	single-minded	it is possible	Self	this	form	

ज्ञातुं	द्रष्टुं	चा	तत्त्वेन	प्रवेष्टुं	च	परन्तप
jnaatum	drashtuM	ca	tattvena	praveshtum	ca	parantapa
to be known	seen	and	in reality	be entered into	and	destroyer of foes

By unswerving, single-minded devotion it is possible for the Self to be known, seen and in reality, be entered and absorbed into.

What if I don't have faith in this process or the end result?

XVII, 3

सत्त्वा	अनुरूपा	सर्वस्य	श्रद्धा	भवति	भारत
sattva	anuruupaa	sarvasya	shraddhaa	bhavati	bhaarata
their nature	in accordance	of all beings	faith	is	Bharata

श्रद्धामयः	अयं	पुरुषः	यः	यच्छ्रद्धः	सः	एव	सः
shraddhaamayaH	ayam	purushaH	yah	yacchraddhaH	saH	eva	saH
made up of faith	this	person	who	whatever faith is he	indeed	is	that

The faith of everyone is according to their inherent nature, their natural temperament. A person is basically made up of his faith. As his faith is, so indeed is he. His life is shaped by his faith.

Whether or not you will be drawn to a spiritual practice, how seriously you will practice it, and whether or not you will ultimately be willing to surrender your "I/ego", will be determined by your faith which is in turn determined on your "true nature". This true nature is determined by your genetics, conditioning, environment, when and where you were born, your friends, etc. The fact that you are reading this now is itself a demonstration of your tendencies and faith.

28

IV, 39

श्रद्धावान	लभते	ज्ञानं	तत्परः	संयत	इन्द्रियः
shraddhaavaan	labhate	jnaanam	tatparaH	samyata	indriyaH
one who has faith	attains	knowledge	is diligent	has control of	his senses

ज्ञानं	लब्ध्वा	परां	शान्तिम्	अचिरेण	अधिगच्छति
jnaanam	labdhvaa	paraam	shaantim	acirena	adhigacchati
knowledge	attaining	absolute	peace	soon	gains

One who has faith and diligence, and who has control of his senses, attains knowledge. Having attained this knowledge, (s)he soon reaches the state of absolute Peace.

If you have faith, and diligence, and the ability to control your responses to your sensations and desires, you will gain the requisite knowledge and understanding and will quickly attain the absolute peace that "passeth understanding", the Self.

IF I'M FOCUSED ON AWAKENING CAN THAT BE ENOUGH?

X, 10

तेषां	सतत	युक्तानां	भजतां	प्रीति	पुउर्वकं
teshaam	satata	yuktaanaam	bhajataam	priiti	puurvakam
for those	always	devoted to Self	who worship	love	with

ददामि	बुद्धि	योगं	तं	येन	मां	उपयान्ति	ते
dadaami	buddhi	yogam	tam	yena	maam	upayaanti	te
I give	wisdom	possession	that	by which	Self	reach	they

To those who are always devoted to and worship the Self with love, I give the possession of wisdom by which they can reach the Self.

X, 11

तेषां	एव	अनुकम्पार्थं	अहम्	अज्ञानजं	तमः
teshaam	eva-	anukampaartham	aham	ajnaanajam	tamaH
for them	alone	out of compassion	Self	born of ignorance	delusion

30

नाशयामि	आत्म	भावः	स्थः	ज्ञान	दीपेन	भास्वता
naashayaami	aatma	bhaavaH	sthaH	jnana	diipena	bhaasvataa
destroy	in their hearts	seat	abiding	knowledge	lamp	luminous

Out of compassion for them alone, Self, abiding in their hearts, destroys the delusion born of ignorance with the luminous lamp of knowledge.

V, 16

ज्ञानेन	तु	तत्	अज्ञानं	येषां	नाशितं	आत्मनः
jnaanena	tu	tat	ajnaanam	yeshaam	naashitam-	aatmanaH
by knowledge	but	that	ignorance	whose	is destroyed	of the Self

तेषाम्	आदित्यवत्	ज्ञानं	प्रकाशयति	तत्	परम्
teshaam	aadityavat	jnaanam	prakaashayati	tat	param
their	like the sun	knowledge	reveals	that	Self

But for those whose ignorance is destroyed by knowledge of the Self, their knowledge, like the sun, reveals that Self.

The classical metaphor from Ramana Maharshi is that one should desire awakening "like one being held underwater". Some Zen folk use the example of "like having your hair on fire". Our regional zendo, at which i was one of the two principal leaders for a while, had a painting of a man with his hair on fire to keep that example present in the sitters' awareness.

If one has great dedication and lasting devotion to awakening, with all their heart, in my experience, they will invariably find the truth. This is described here as compassion for them, manifesting through the Self, which yields discrimination and understanding. This luminous lamp of knowledge, abiding in every thought, will destroy the darkness born of ignorance, like the sun, and reveal the supreme stillness of the Self.

31

WHAT SHOULD I DO ABOUT MY DESIRES?

III, 33

सद्रशं	चेष्टते	स्वस्याः	प्रक्रतेः	ज्ञानवान्	अपि
sadrsham	ceshtate	svasyaaH	prakrteH	jnaanavaan	api
in keeping with	acts	of one's own	nature	a wise person	even

प्रक्रितं	यान्ति	भूतानि	निग्रहः	किं	करिष्यति
prakrtim	yaanti	bhuutaani	nigrahaH	kiM	karishyati
nature	follow	beings	restraint	what	will accomplish

Even a (wo)man of wisdom acts in accordance with their own nature. Beings follow their nature. What will restraint accomplish?

This is a seldom cited verse, as in a religious context, taken at face value, it can easily be interpreted as saying there is nothing one can do but accept the attractions of the senses and go with the flow of the desires that arise.

That is not the intent of this section, however, as the following verse (III, 34) says that one should not come under the sway of the senses as they are his foe/enemy. Seven verses follow describing how destructive unrestrained desire is to spiritual development employing metaphors like a great devourer, a cloud like dirt on a mirror, insatiable fire, veiling Knowledge, and a destroyer of learning and wisdom.

The next two verses offer the resolution in an elegant, logical, approach.

III, 42

इन्द्रियाणि	पराणि	आहुः	इन्द्रियेभ्यः	परं	मनः
indriyaani	*paraani*	*aahuH*	*indriyebhyaH*	*param*	*manaH*
senses	superior	they say	to the senses	superior	mind

मनसः	तु	परा	बुद्धिः	यः	बुद्धेः	परतः	तु	सः
manasaH	*tu*	*paraa*	*buddhiH*	*yaH*	*buddheH*	*parataH*	*tu*	*saH*
to mind	but	superior	intellect	who	to intellect	superior	but	Self

They say that the senses are superior (to the body); the mind is superior to the senses; the intellect is superior to the mind, but what is superior to the intellect is Self.

III, 43

एवं	बुद्धेः	परं	बुद्वा	संस्तभ्य	अत्मानं	आत्मना
evam	*buddheH*	*param*	*buddhvaa*	*samstabhya*	*atmaanam*	*aatmanaa*
thus	to intellect	superior	understanding	establishing	Self	with the mind

जहि	शत्रुं	महा	बाहो	काम	रूपं	दुर्	आसदं
jahi	*shatrum*	*mahaa*	*baaho*	*kaama*	*ruupam*	*dur*	*aasadam*
destroy	enemy	mighty	armed	desire	the form of	hard	to subdue

33

Understanding that the Self is superior to the intellect, (which is superior to the mind, and it to the senses and they to the body), establish yourself in the Self by controlling each of these with the next higher one with the help of the mind. This will destroy the enemy manifesting in the form of desire which is difficult to subdue.

For me, this boils down to surrendering the I/ego, which is the driving force behind self-referential desires, to the Self. Without the energy of the "flywheel" of the I/me/my driving the desires into craving, what remains is only the organic essence of desire. It is surprising how much desire is reduced when self-referential thoughts fall away.

WHAT ROLE DOES RENUNCIATION HAVE IN YOGA?

VI, 2

यं	संन्यासं	इति	प्राहुः	योगं	तं	विद्धि	पाण्डव
yam	sannyaasam	iti	praahuH	yogaM	taM	viddhi	paandava
that which	renunciation	thus	call	yoga	that	know	Arjuna

न	हि	अ	संन्यस्त	संकल्पः		योगी	भवति	कश्चन
na	hi	a-	sannyasta	sankalpaH		yogii	bhavati	kashcana
not	verily	not	renouncing	thoughts of results		yogi	become	anyone

That which they call renunciation, know that to be yoga. Verily, anyone who has not given up thoughts of results is not a yogi.

"Thoughts of results" here is one interpretation; others translate "sankalpaH" as "expectation or anticipation of results" or simply "thoughts". This approach of renouncing any expectations or thoughts of results from one's actions, is really the basis of Karma Yoga.

It is really striking to see how much the quality and nature of "doing" changes when the results of whatever actions are being

35

done are completely surrendered. The clarity and skill with which the actions are performed is greatly enhanced when there is no attachment to the outcome. IME, this is action of a wholly different character and creativity.

How does practice change as one progresses?

VI, 3

आरुरुक्षोः	मुनेः	योगं	कर्म	कारणं	उच्यते
aarurukshoH	muneH	yogam	karma	kaaranam	ucyate
wishing to attain	for sage	to yoga	action	means	is said to be

योग	आरूउदस्य	तस्य	एव	शमः	कारणं	उच्यते
yoga	aaruudasya	tasya	eva	shamaH	kaaranam	ucyate
Yoga	one who attains	for him	alone	inaction	means	is said to be

For a sage who has been unable to remain established in Jnana Yoga, performing action without regard for the results, or Karma Yoga, is said to be the means.

For a sage who has been able to remain established in Jnana Yoga, withdrawal from actions, or inaction, is said to be the means.

The "withdrawal from actions" can also be interpreted as abiding in stillness with actions occurring without a "doer", even as one appears to be involved in the world. As the Gita, IV, 18 states: "He who finds inaction in action and action in inaction, he is the wise one among men; he is engaged in yoga and is a performer of all actions!"

This "doing" without a "doer" is what is meant by action in inaction; there is nothing being "done" by anyone, so there is inaction as far as an agent is concerned, but "things" still happen, wood still gets chopped and water carried.

Inaction in action is what occurs when there is someone "doing" something to get a desired result. The doer obscures the "doing" with his fixation on the reward from the action, so there is no real clarity in the action, which is inaction.

Is there any hope for me, I have done some really bad things?

IV, 36

अपि	चेत	सि	पापेभ्यः	सर्वेभ्यः	पापक्रत्तमः
api	*cet*	*asi*	*paapebhyaH*	*sarvebhyaH*	*paapakrttamaH*
even	if	you are	sinners	among all	the worst sinner

सर्व	ज्ञान	प्लवेन	एव	वृजिनं	सन्तरिष्यसि
sarvam	*jnaana*	*plavena*	*eva*	*vrjinam*	*santarishyasi*
all	knowledge	by the raft	alone	wickedness	you will cross over

Even if you are the worst of all sinners, you will cross over all those sins with just the raft of knowledge.

There is also the sense that "righteousness", in the form of formal religious observance, is an "evil" if one is aspiring to directly realize the Self. Knowledge is the raft; religious observance is the water to be crossed over.

This is a reassuring, almost "Christian", verse and sets up the next verses which discuss how this "raft" of knowledge can become a "fire" of knowledge to remove the results of those past actions.

HOW CAN I GET FREE OF THE RESULTS OF MY ACTIONS?

IV, 37

यथा	एधांसि	समिद्धः	अग्निः	भस्मसात्	कुरुते	अर्जुन
yathaa	edhaamsi	samiddhaH	agniH	bhasmasaat	kurute	Arjuna
just as	sticks of wood	blazing	fire	to ashes	reduces	Arjuna

ज्ञान	अग्निः	सर्व	कर्माणि	भस्मसात्	कुरुते	तथा
jnaana	agniH	sarva	karmaani	bhasmasaat	kurute	tathaa
knowledge	fire	all	actions	to ashes	reduces	so too

As a blazing fire reduces sticks of wood to ashes, so too does the fire of knowledge reduce the results of all actions to ashes.

All of the stories, guilt and blame related to our past actions, and whether they were believed to be good or bad, honorable or sinful, disappear with the understanding that there was never any doer, nor was there any possibility for it to have occurred any other way. We have no ability to predict the future results of any of our actions or even who they will affect, in what way and in what events and activities. Understanding this, how can we feel proud, sorry or angry for any actions?

As we will see in later verses, "i do nothing at all."

IV, 19

यस्य	सर्वे	समारम्भाः	काम	संकल्प		वर्जितः
yasya	sarve	samaarambhah	kaama	sankalpa		varjitah
for whom	all	undertakings	desire	thoughts of results		free

ज्ञान	अग्निः	दग्ध	कर्माणं	तं	आहुः	पण्डितं	बुधाः
jnaana	agniH	dagdha	karmaanam	tam	aahuh	panditam	budhaah
knowledge	fire	burned	whose actions	him	call	wise	the sages

One whose undertakings are all free from desire and thoughts of results, and whose actions have been burned in the flame of knowledge is called wise by the sages.

This echoes the earlier verse, VI, 2, of renouncing the results of any of our actions even as they are done, which is the essence of Karma Yoga.

WHAT EFFECT DOES MY CONTROL OF MY THOUGHTS HAVE?

V, 26

काम	क्रोध	वियुक्तानां	यतीनां		यत	चेतसां
kaama	krodha	viyuktaanaam	yatinaam		yata	cetasaam
desire	anger	free from	for aspirants		who	controlled thoughts

अभितः	ब्रह्म	निर्वाणं	वर्तते	विदित	आत्मनाम्
abhitaH	brahma	nirvaanam	vartate	vidita	aatmanaam
living or dead		liberation	there is	who know	the Self

For those aspirants who are free from desire and anger, who have controlled their thoughts, and who know the Self, there is absorption and liberation, whether the body is alive or dead, here now or hereafter.

42

WHAT PRACTICE, WHAT APPROACH, SHOULD I USE TO REACH THE SELF?

VI, 25

शनैः	शनैः	उपरमेत्	बुद्धया	धृति	ग्रहीतया
shanaiH	shanaiH	uparamet	buddhyaa	dhrti	grhiitayaa
slowly	slowly	withdraw	with the intellect	steadiness	endowed

आत्म	संस्थं	मनः	कृत्वा	न	किञ्चित्	अपि	चिन्तयेत्
aatma	saMstham	manaH	krtvaa	na	kincit	api	cintayet
in the Self	fixed	mind	making	not	anything	whatsoever	think

One should gradually, gradually, attain stillness, with an intellect endowed with steadiness. Fixing the mind in the Self, (with the idea "The Self alone is all; there is nothing apart from It") one should not think of anything whatsoever.

Shankara, the great codifier of Advaita Vedanta/nonduality, has said about this verse, "This is the highest instruction about Yoga." It is about as compact and "tight" as one could imagine for a description of the process used to accomplish nondual absorption and abiding in stillness without thoughts.

Patanjali, the codifier of yoga w/his famous "Yoga Sutras", defines "yoga" in the second sutra of the 196 sutras, as "yogash citta vrtti nirodhaH". This is frequently translated as "yoga is the stilling of the modifications of the mind", almost identical to Shankara's interpretation of this verse in the Gita. It is so very simple, just "make the mind fixed in the Self without thinking of anything". Simple, as we all know, is not the same as easy.

One may also be able to train the mind to such an extent that it can be suppressed with different meditation approaches so that thoughts do not arise. However, this is not true nondual awakening; this is just intense concentration and suppression.

This intense suppression requires a highly-trained "doer", the very opposite of what is required for nondual awakening. When thoughts stop because the "I"/doer has been deconstructed and absorbed, so that there is no I/me/my to manifest self-referential thoughts, then what is known as "sahaj", or natural, "nirvikalpa samadhi", thoughtless absorption, arises.

The really good news is, as J. Krishnamurti pointed out, that the brain "does not want" to be confused, chaotic and disordered; it wants to be ordered, clear and present. There is of course, no anthropomorphized "wanting", but in my experience, the sustained, easy, heightened, thought-free, presence and stillness is the result of the brain's strong "preference" for this state.

Ultimately, it comes down to the brain's choosing between stillness and "monkey mind". If we give it enough "data" through frequent, even if brief, glimpses of thoughtless presence, it will refunctionalize into an effortless pattern without an I/me/my as its standard operating system.

In my experience, the brain so strongly prefers this stillness and presence, that, with time, it is unnecessary to reject "pleasures" or self-referential desires, thoughts and fears; they are simply not attractive to the brain. The preference can be so strong that experienced nondual practitioners often find it really uncomfortable to move into self-referential thoughts, desires and fears.

As Ramana Maharshi pointed out in his "Talks", "It will then become difficult to even create thoughts."

The work on meditation and brain refunctionalization as in Farb, et al. (2007) shows that all of the brains, even in as short a period as 45 mins/day for 2 months of mindfulness meditation, solved the problem in the same way. All of the brains preferred "now, now, now" to the customary default of "blah, blah, blah" self-referential narrative, and refunctionalized in the same new, altered pattern to support that preference.

VI, 26

यतः	यतः	निश्चरति	मनः	चञ्चलं	अस्थिरं
yataH	yataH	nishcarati	manaH	cancalam	asthiram
for whatever reason		wanders away	mind	restless	unsteady

ततः	ततः	नियम्य	एतत्	आत्मनि	एव	वशं	नयेत्
tataH	tataH	niyamya	etat	aatmani	eva	vasham	nayet
from those causes		restraining	it	of the Self	itself	under control	bring

For whatever reason, distraction or object, when the restless, unsteady mind wanders away, restrain it from those causes, and bring it under the control of the Self itself.

This verse is a good complement to its predecessor in the Gita, cited above. An important implication of this verse is that the "reason" that the restless, unsteady mind has wandered away is of no significance, it is just "yataH, yataH" (yada, yada) and "tataH, tataH" which translate literally as "due to whatever objects" and "from all those causes whatever", respectively. The focus of attention in nondual meditation is on the Self, not on whatever might have distracted the wayward mind. If the mind

45

strays off to "whatever", bring it back under control of, and into, the Self.

As Ramana Maharshi pointed out in "Who Am I?" in response to the question "Is it necessary for one who longs for liberation to inquire into the nature of categories?"

Just as one who wants to throw away garbage has no need to analyze it and see what it is, so one who wants to know the Self has no need to count the number of categories or inquire into their characteristics; what he has to do is to reject altogether the categories that hide the Self.

WHAT NEEDS TO BE ACCOMPLISHED FOR ME TO BE "LIBERATED"?

V, 28

यत	इन्द्रियः	मनः	बुद्धिः	मुनिर्	मोक्ष	परायणः
yata	indriyaH	manaH	buddhiH	muniH	moksha	paraayanaH
mastered	senses	mind	intellect	wise one	awakening	fully intent on

विगतः	इच्छा	भय	क्रोदः	यः	सदा	मुक्त	एव	सः
vigataH	icchaa	bhaya	krodhaH	yaH	sadaa	mukta	eva	saH
one free	desire	fear	anger	who	always	liberated	indeed	he

Having mastered the senses, mind and intellect, the wise one is fully intent on awakening. (S)he who is always without desire, fear or anger is indeed liberated.

The last part of the second line is translated two different ways, about equally often by good sources. It can be taken as "one who is always free from desire, fear and anger is indeed liberated", or it can be translated as "one who is free from desire, fear and anger, is indeed forever liberated." Both work.

A useful distinction is between emotions and their self-referentially enhanced versions, i.e. between anger and rage, desire and lust, and fear and terror. Completely shutting down any movement of consciousness into "useful" fears which prevent things like stepping off a cliff or in front of a bus is not what is intended, only eliminating the mentally-enhanced movement into anticipatatory terror.

How will "others" appear when "I" am absorbed in the Self?

VI, 29

सर्व	भूत	स्थं	आत्मानं	सर्व	भूतानि	च	आत्मनि
sarva	bhuuta	stham	aatmaanam	sarva	bhuutaani	ca	aatmani
all	beings	existing in	the Self	all	beings	and	in the Self

ईक्शते	योग	युक्त	आत्मा	सर्वत्र	समा	दर्शनः
iikshate	yoga	yukta	aatmaa	sarvatra	sama	darshanaH
sees	through yoga	absorbed in	the Self	everywhere	same	has vision

Through yoga, one whose mind is absorbed in the Self, sees the Self existing in all beings (and everything) and all beings (and everything) existing in the Self, sees the same thing everywhere.

There are two different ways to interpret this wonderful verse, both powerful. The simpler interpretation is that one sees the Self in all beings (and everything) and sees all beings (and everything) in the Self, i.e. Brahman is in everything and everything is in Brahman. In this interpretation it is possible to fall into a philosophical situation with one standing outside and seeing Brahman in everything, and everything in Brahman, i.e. me here, seeing Brahman out there, and there and there and all of those things in Brahman, etc.

49

A more interesting and powerful interpretation, in my humble opinion, is the next logical step, which is differentiated philosophically. That is that if one is absorbed in the Self, that one sees Self as everything and everything as Self. This "feels" more like what is ultimately experienced. The Self, Brahman, isn't something "out there" that has these properties, but you, personally and actually, are totally absorbed in/as the Self. The Self isn't outside of you, it is you, except that you aren't there, you are everything and everything is you. Logically, for you to be everything, "you" must not exist discretely and separately.

There is also the timeless introduction to the Isha Upanishad:

This is fullness. That is fullness. From that fullness this fullness came. From that fullness, if this fullness is removed, what remains is only fullness.

The first line in Hakuin's famous *Song of Zazen*, which when i read it in graduate school was the verse that opened "me" dramatically into a dimension i had no idea even existed, is similar:

All beings are from the very beginning Buddhas.

This really is what manifests. It was surprising, but was so totally "right" and "yes", when it manifested. While everything can still be differentiated by the senses, there is the deep knowing, "seeing" and understanding that they are all One; everything is Oneness and Oneness is everything.

This moves easily into the next verse.

If I fully surrender will the body be safe?

IX, 22

अनन्यः	चिन्तयन्तः	मां	ये	जनः	पर्युपासते
ananyaH	cintayantaH	maam	ye	janah	paryupaasate
not different	meditate on	the Self	those	people	worship everywhere

तेषां	नित्य	अभियुक्तानां	योग	क्षेमं	वहामि	अहं
tesham	nitya	abhiyuktaanaam	yoga	kshemam	vahaami	aham
for them	always	attached to	need	preserve	arrange for	Self

For those who worship/see the Self everywhere, meditate on the Self, and are always united with and attached to the Self, the Self provides what they need and preserves and protects what they have.

This is one of the most frequently quoted verses in the Bhagavad Gita. It is also one that causes doubt to arise for some as to the reasonableness and likelihood of this being true. Is it just another hopeful "religious" promise that folk desperately cling to, but which has no real validity?

To my great astonishment, this has proven to be unfailingly true, so much so that it has been a primary "proof" that there is "something there" (or "here") and that the path itself is real and

51

true. The more that "I" surrendered, the more there was the deep feeling, the deep knowing with certainty, that "I" was being held, almost literally, in the hand of "something". When a little was surrendered, there was a little feeling of support; when more and more was surrendered, there was more and more a deep certainty of being held and protected. When complete surrender occurred, there was Self everywhere and freedom.

Although "I" discovered this empirically "all by myself", Ajahn Chah stated a similar thing:

If you let go a little, you will have a little happiness.

If you let go a lot, you will have a lot of happiness.

If you let go completely, you will be free.

The next verse extends and reinforces this concept.

VII, 17

तेषां	ज्ञानी		नित्य	युक्तः	एक	भक्तिः	विशिष्यते
teshaaM	jnaanii		nitya	yuktaH	eka	bhaktiH	vishishyate
of them	knower of Reality		always	steadfast	Self	devotion to	excels

प्रियः	हि	ज्ञानिनः	अत्यर्थं	अहं	सः	च	मम	प्रियः
priyaH	hi	jnaaninaH	atyartham	aham	saH	ca	mama	priyaH
beloved	since	by knower	very much	the Self	he	and	to Self	beloved

Of them, the knower of Reality, who is always steadfast and devoted to the Self, excels. Since the Self is "very much" beloved by the knower of Reality, he too is beloved to/by the Self.

"Knowledge" is often used in place of "Reality", and capitalized, to signify not mere accumulation of information, but rather a complete deep understanding.

The "of them" is addressing the four categories of seekers, "people of virtuous deeds", described in the preceding Gita verse, VII, 16. These are a) the afflicted who are overcome by sorry, distress and disease, etc., b) the seeker of knowledge who wants to know the Reality, c) the seeker of wealth, and d) the man of knowledge who possesses intellectual knowledge but now wants to truly know the Self.

In the following verse in the Gita, VII, 18, the question is asked, "What happens to the other three classes of seekers?" The reply is "All of these three, indeed, are noble, but the knower of Reality, the man of Knowledge, is the very Self."

The next verse, VII, 19 gives an indication of just how often there is someone who "truly knows the Self".

How often does someone "reach the Self"?

VII, 19

बहूनां	जन्मनां	अन्ते	ज्ञानवान्	मां	प्रपद्यते
bahuunaaM	janmanaam	ante	jnaanavaan	maaM	prapadyate
many	births	after	man of Knowledge	the Self	attains

वासुदेवः	सर्वं	इति	सः	महा	आत्मा	सु	दुर्लभः
vaasudevaH	sarvam	iti	saH	maha	aatmaa	su-	durlabhaH
The Self	all	that	such a	great	soul	very	rare

After many births, the man of Knowledge attains the Self, realizing that the Self is all. Such a great soul is very rare.

"Births" can be interpreted in different ways. They can be the birth and death and rebirth of the physical body, which is how this is traditionally interpreted.

Another interpretation is that in the course of one's spiritual efforts the "I" goes through many deaths and births, and changes as it is disassembled into a modified and less concrete "improved" version, over and over again.

54

It can also be taken to be the death and birth of the ad-hoc "I" from relationship to relationship, or meeting to meeting, as one goes through a typical day and encounters other folk. If you watch carefully, you can see that a different "I" shows up for each different folk and then dies away before the next meeting occurs or even as as others arrive at or leave the meeting. As Virginia Woolf, the famous English writer observed, "One has as many 'I's as they have relationships."

A useful approach to see this directly is to ask "When am I?" repeatedly throughout your day. See if "you" are there all the time and if you are the same "you" all the time. It may become clear that "you" are really an ad hoc construct that is born, dies and is reborn continuously, until it is clearly seen, and then falls away.

VII, 3

मनुष्याणां	सहस्रेषु	कश्चित्	यतति	सिद्धये
manushyaanaaM	sahasreshu	kashcit	yatati	siddhaye
of people	among thousands	rare one	strives	for perfection

यततां	अपि	सिद्धानां	कश्चित्	मां	वेत्ति	तत्त्वतः
yatataam	api	siddhaanaaM	kashcit	maam	vetti	tattvataH
who strive	even	among those	perhaps one	the Self	knows	in truth

Among thousands of (wo)men, the rare one strives for perfection; even among those who strive, perhaps one knows the Self, in truth.

Most translations leave the last line as it is, literally. Others have added some inferred statistics in the line, by translating it as "even among those who strive, only one in a thousand, in truth...". This would make it roughly one in a million folk who would "in truth, know the Self".

Others, presumably uncomfortable with the literal translation that only ONE will know the truth, have changed it to "only a few". Since the same Sanskrit term is used in both lines, "only the few" can be substituted in both lines, so that it becomes, "Among thousands of (wo)men, only a few strive for perfection; even among those who strive, only a few, in truth, know the Self." This would seem to be a more useful translation than the traditional ones.

Whatever translation you embrace, given these two verses, the odds are not very high that many folk, certainly not most folk, will "realize the Self". This has troubled many who hope that much of humankind will come to nondual awakening at some time in the future. There is, of course, no way to know exactly what the number was, or is, at any time accurately, but there is little doubt that in the intervening two and a half millennia, not many have come to "in truth, know the Self". Perhaps with our vastly superior mass communication capabilities, interconnectivity and availability of the teachings for all, this will change.

It is also important to understand that "realizing the Self" is not a destination, but an unfolding process, even after deep understanding and absorption has manifested. As Harada Roshi, one of the great Zen masters of the 19th and 20th century stated, "Enlightenment is capable of endless enlargement." If someone tells you that they are "enlightened", look more deeply; ask them just who it is that it is enlightened. Also, if someone says to "call of the search" for awakening, and tells you that you're already enlightened, ask them who it is that is so anxious to call off the search.

This may leave us in a down-hearted state at our odds, and at the odds of humankind's "knowing the Self". However, the next verse offers a more optimistic outlook.

BUT SOME ARE SUCCESSFUL IN "REACHING THE SELF"...

IV, 10

विइत	राग	भय	क्रोधः	मन्मयाः	मां	उपाश्रिताः
vita	raaga	bhaya	krodhaaH	manmayaaH	maam	upaashritaaH
free	attachment	fear	anger	absorbed in Self	in Self	taking refuge

बहवः	ज्ञान	तपसा	पूताः	मद्भावं	आगताः
bahavaH	jnaana	tapasaa	puutaaH	madbhaavam	aagataaH
many	knowledge	fire	purified	the state of Self	have attained

Free from attachment, fear and anger, totally absorbed in the Self, taking refuge in the Self, purified by the fire of knowledge, many have returned to, and attained the Self.

So, "attaining the Self" is achievable if one has attained certain levels of spiritual development. With sufficient desire, it can be done. As the famous quote from Shankara's Vivekachudamani attests, "The most important qualification for Liberation is the desire for Liberation." This is echoed in Ramana Maharshi's quote "The successful few owe their success to their persistence." Even the contemporary Adyashanti echoes a similar sentiment with his observation that if he sees someone who "must" awaken, they will. That has been my experience, as well.

i knew that "awakening" was the reason "i" was here and that it was the most important thing to do in this life. i didn't even really know what "enlightenment" was, and my religious training told me it was impossible, even heretical, but I knew it could be done and that i must do it.

WHY SHOULD I GIVE UP MY DESIRES?

II, 55

प्रजहाति	यदा	कामान्	सर्वान्	पार्थ	मनोगतान्
prajahaati	yadaa	kaamaan	sarvaan	paartha	manogataan
fully gives up	when	desires	all	Arjuna	that enter the mind

आत्मनि	एव	आत्मना	तुष्टः	स्थित	प्राज्ञः	तदा	उच्यते
aatmani	eva	aatmanaa	tushtaH	sthita	prajnaH	tadaa	ucyate
in the Self	only	by the Self	satisfied	steady	wisdom	then	is called

When one fully, completely, gives up all desires that enter the mind, and is satisfied only with the Self and by the Self, then (s)he is called a (wo)man of steady wisdom.

The first line, taken by itself, leaves one in a presumably dire situation. Some folk are concerned that having given up all desires, including the desire for food, shelter and clothing, and having nothing to give one satisfaction, one may well "lose one's power of discrimination" and behave recklessly and indiscriminately and may injure or destroy the body.

However, as the second line points out, this need for feeling and experiencing satisfaction is fulfilled by being satisfied by the Self and with the Self, alone. i have characterized this state as being such that there is nothing that could be added or taken away that

59

would improve it in any way. It is really "complete" in the fullest sense of the word. This makes one stable with steady wisdom. There is no place else one would rather be, so one is only "here and now". The last part can also be translated as "...and is happy by oneself, in one's Self alone..."

The "awakened" state is not some empty, terrifying "Void", or "emptiness" as it is often translated and characterized in some famous Buddhist texts and elsewhere. It is ultimately the most blissful state one can experience. Working with many folk has anecdotally shown that folk consistently rank the "typical level of pleasure" for the persistent nondual state higher than psychedelics and both of those higher than sex. The next lower state is the typical dualistic state after one has experienced the nondual state; the lowest is the typical dualistic state.

In my experience, if one surrenders the "I", the self-referential desires, which are not necessary to sustain the body, do fall away. One still experiences thirst, hunger, cold, heat, pain, etc., so the physical body is maintained; fundamental protective responses still occur and nerve endings don't vanish. You do not suddenly walk off a cliff or step in front of a bus.

What is lost is the "flywheel of suffering" generated by a self-referential ego/I with its narrative, memories and projections - protective pain turns into suffering, basic bodily needs turn into craving and greed, etc.

This "(wo)man of steady wisdom" gains benefits from his/her renunciation of desire, as explained in the next verse.

II, 71

विहाय	कामान्	यः	सर्वान्	पुमां		चारति	निःस्पृहः
vihaaya	kaamaan	yaH	sarvaan	pumaan		carati	niHsprhaH
after rejecting	desires	who	all		knower of Self	moves	without longing

निर्	ममः	निर्	अहन्कारः	सः	शान्तिं	अधि	गच्छति
nir -	mamaH	nir -	ahankaaraH	saH	shaantim	adhi-	gacchati
w/o	sense of mine	w/o	the "I"	he	peace		attains

The one who knows the Self, the (wo)man of steady wisdom, who has given up all desires, moves about without longing, without the sense of "I" and mine, and attains peace and the end of suffering.

Some traditions focus on the practice of not indulging in any and all desires. In my experience, that approach doesn't work. Forcefully trying to suppress all desires often results in deep conflict, confusion, torment and sometimes, extreme reactions and behaviors. Many are simply unable to do it, despite the exhortations of scriptures, priests, institutions, etc. The basic structure of self-referential desire has not been changed.

In the direct, nondual approach, deconstructing the sense of "I" and "mine" using meditative inquiry, "changes the game". Self-referential thoughts, desires, and fears are dramatically weakened or disappear. Simple sensations cannot expand into problems without an "I" or "mine" to energize and perpetuate them. There is no "flywheel of suffering". A decades-long habitual user of cannabis, with whom i did this work, lost all craving for cannabis simply by asking, repeatedly, "Who would smoke it?"

WHAT SHOULD I DO ABOUT "FIXING" THE WORLD?

XII, 15

यस्मात्	न	उद्विजते	लोकः	लोकात्		न	उद्विजते	चा	यः
yasmaat	na	udvijate	lokaH	lokaat		na-	udvijate	ca	yaH
by whom	not	is disturbed	world	by the world		not	is disturbed	and	who

हर्ष	अमर्ष		भय	उद्वेगैः	मुक्तः	यः	स	चा	मे	प्रियः
harsha	amarsha		bhaya	udvegaiH	muktaH	yaH	sa	ca	me	priyaH
elation	intolerance	fear	anxiety	free		who	he	and	Me	beloved to

He by whom the world is not disturbed and who is not disturbed by the world, he who is free from elation, intolerance, fear and anxiety, is beloved by the Self.

This is obviously not the prevailing sentiment among those who feel it is their personal mission to save the world or mankind. To be told that you are not to be disturbed by the world "situation", and thereby, to not feel that you are responsible for fixing it, can be disconcerting, at the least.

The most direct approach is to focus on your own "world situation", rather than the "external" world, and fix "yourself" first. If you are impatient, fearful, lost in your never-ending search for great(er) pleasure, worried and anxious, how can you bring intelligent and appropriate action to "fix the world"? Are you merely hiding from your fears and anxieties by focusing on fixing everything else, rather than dealing with the real problem?

The nondual, awakened, approach is to realize through self-inquiry that "you", in fact, are the world and that "everything is One". If you reach this state, you will find that not only are you more "beloved by the Self", but also that the world seems now to be doing much better, thank you. You will also find that your actions, arising from the Self, really are helping "the world" in ways you could never have imagined.

There is also the non-dualistic approach expressed by 20th century (and earlier) sages, like Ramana Maharshi and Nisargadatta Majaraj, as well as contemporary teachers like the Zen teacher, Adyashanti. They say that if you really understood how powerful your awakening was to the energy of the world, and were really serious about "fixing" the world, you would work on nothing else.

"If you, who have come to this world alone...subside in Self by knowing what is the reality of yourself, know that that is the greatest help which you can render to all the other people in this world."

Ramana Maharshi

How do I deal with changes
in my moods?

XIV, 22

प्रकाशं	च	प्रवृत्तिं	चा	मोहं	एव	च	पाण्डव
prakaasham	ca	pravrittiM	ca	moham	eva	ca	paandava
illumination	and	activity	and	delusion	even	and	Arjuna

न	द्वेष्टि	संप्रव्त्तानि	न	निव्त्तानि	काङ्क्षति
na	dveshti	sampravrttaani	na	nivrttaani	kaankshati
not	dislike them	when appear	nor	when they disappear	long for them

When illumination, activity and delusion appear, he does not dislike them, nor does he long for them when they disappear.

This verse is in response to the previous verse, XIV, 21, which asks "By what signs is one known who has gone beyond these three qualities (gunas)? What is his behavior, and how does he transcend these three qualities?"

As described in XIV, 5, such a person is called a *"guna-atiitaH"*, or one who has "transcended (*atiitaH*) the three qualities – *sattva* (knowledge, happiness), *rajas* (passion, attachment, desire) and *tamas* (inertia, laziness, ignorance, lack of discrimination) which "bind the immutable embodied being to the body".

The entire fourteenth verse of the Gita is focused on The Three Gunas, and how to transcend them, how to go beyond the "field" and the "knower of the field" discussed earlier, to reach a transcendent state.

"Prakaasham" is associated with the sattva guna; "pravrittim" with the rajas guna, and "moham" with the tamas guna. If one transcends them all, even as they do their inevitable dance, one does not dislike any particular one of them when they arise, nor does (s)he long for one which has gone away.

This is a very easy verse to misinterpret. There is so much focus placed on reaching a sattvic state so that one is not buffeted by the dance of rajas/activity and tamas/laziness/inertia, that it is often viewed as the ultimate attainment. This verse emphasizes that even sattva, in the form of the illumination arising from knowledge, is also binding as one becomes attached to the realization. Complete transcendence goes beyond attachment to even the sattvic state.

How this transcendence of the three gunas manifests in reality is seen in the next verse.

How about when others dislike or disrespect me?

XIV, 25

मान	अपमानयोः	तुल्यः	तुल्यः	मित्र	अरि	पक्षयोः
maana	apamaanayoH	tulyaH	tulyaH	mitra	ari	pakshayoH
respect	disrespect	the same	the same	friend	enemy	their views

सर्व	आरम्भः	परित्यागी	गुणाः	अतिइतः	सः	उच्यते
sarva	aarambhaH	parityaagii	gunaaH	atiitaH	saH	ucyate
all	undertakings	renounced	gunas	beyond	he	is called

(s)he who is the same whether (s)he is regarded with respect or disrespect, who has the same attitude towards the views of both friends and enemies, who has no sense of ownership or doership in undertakings – (s)he is said to have transcended the qualities/gunas (and become a guna-atiitaH).

"Abandons the initiative in all undertakings" is also translated more classically as "abandoning all undertakings" or "given up all undertakings". A more contemporary interpretation would be "given up the desire for, and sense of doership/ownership of the results of all activities".

The "abandons the initiative..." interpretation is the one preferred by Ramana Maharshi; he never encouraged anyone to abandon all undertakings or activities. Despite the fact that he spent 17 years mostly in silence in Virupaksha cave, Ramana said that one should continue working where one is, and not retire to the cave or jungle, as the difficulties would only increase there. It is better to just let go of one's attachment to the work, and do whatever it is that comes to you without feeling that it is MY work.

Ramana, himself, was very active in "the undertakings" of the ashram. As detailed extensively in the biography of one of his closest followers, Annamalai Swami, in "Living By The Words of Bhagavan", Ramana was heavily involved in the daily meal preparations, especially breakfast, and in the construction of the ashram. He and Annamalai Swami, who was the foreman supervising the work for much of the construction and expansion of the ashram's facilities, would meet every morning and evening to plan and then review the results of the day's activities. Ramana was literally the architect of many/most of the buildings in Sri Ramanasramam and was even physically involved in some activities.

IF I BECOME ABSORBED IN THE SELF, WHAT WILL I HAVE TO DO?

III, 17

यः	तु	आत्मा	रतिः	एव	स्यात्	आत्मा	त्रृप्तः	च	मानवः
yah	tu	aatmaa	ratiH	eva	syaat	aatmaa	trptaH	ca	maanavaH
who	but	in Self	rejoices	alone	would be	Self	satisfied	and	man

आत्मनि	एव	च	संतुष्टः	तस्य	कार्यं		न	विद्यते
aatmani	eva	ca	santushtaH	tasya	kaaryaM		na	vidyate
in Self	alone	and	contented	for him	duty to perform		no	there is

But that (wo)man who rejoices only in the Self, is satisfied with the Self, and is content only in the Self – for him/her, there is nothing that has to be done.

The three terms used here refer to different types of pleasures; "ratiH" -attachment to objects, "trptaH" - contact with a particular object, and "santushtaH" - acquisition of a coveted object.

All folk feel contented when they acquire what it is they are craving, but only for a short time until the sensation fades. Then the cycle of loss, desire, longing, craving and searching for a repeat of the previous experience or a better one begins, and the cycle is repeated over and over...

When you truly find the Self, as discussed earlier, you discover that it exceeds the pleasure offered by any object or sensation - you cannot imagine that anything could be added or taken away that would improve this. At that point, you become content and deeply satisfied - there is nothing else to be, do or have.

What our cognitive neuroscience tells us, and what this feels like, is that the brain makes a "benefit/cost ratio" analysis. It wants the most pleasure for the longest time (benefit) with the least pain and distress (cost). As one has pleasurable experiences and recognizes their benefits/costs, the brain develops a good basis for comparison. When the bliss, stillness, order and absorption of the Self is experienced with its lack of perceivable "cost", the brain, naturally, strongly prefers it. If it didn't, our situation would be hopeless and we would be trapped. As discussed earlier, this has been confirmed by comparing the pleasures/ costs of psychedelics, sex and persistent nondual stillness in folk experienced in each; persistent nondual stillness was consistently preferred.

The more experiences that can be had, briefly or over longer times, of Self and the peace that "passeth understanding" with its stillness, presence, etc., the greater will be the brain's ability to refunctionalize its operating patterns. Given enough examples, the brain will optimize its neural network to support remaining in the Self, simply because nothing else compares. It will become natural ("sahaj" in Sanskrit) and easy without any "doing".

It is like learning to ride a bicycle; at first it appears impossible, and if one looks at the brain patterns, there are many regions that are highly activated and engaged. However, with time and repeated attempts, the brain refunctionalizes its patterns so that one can ride a bike with ease, even with no hands, carrying a package, using your phone, etc. There is now only a faint neural activation as the brain is "content" and "satisfied" with this functional pattern.

The same thing happens on the nondual path. Ultimately, that is why there is nothing else to do to abide in the Self. It is nothing mysterious; the brain finds the best state there is and then reorganizes itself to remain in that state. Ultimately, the common report is that it is "almost painful" to move out of that state towards distractions, desires, etc. as the brain prefers it so strongly.

III, 18

नैव	तस्य	क्रतेन	अर्थम्	न	अक्रतेने	ह	कश्चन
naiva	tasya	krtena	artham	na	akrtene	ha	kashcana
not	for him	with doing	concern	nor	not doing	in this world	any

न	चा	अस्य	सर्व	भुउतेषु	कश्चित्	अर्थ	व्यपाश्रयः
na	ca	asya	sarva	bhuuteshu	kashcit	artha	vyapaashrayaH
not	and	for him	all	beings	any	object	dependence on

For him/her, in this world, there is no concern at all with doing or not doing; nor is there any dependence on any being or object for any purpose.

Following on the previous verse, one who is content and totally satisfied with the Self, and who has no particular work to be done, has no purpose for doing or not doing, nor does he depend on anyone, or anything, for any reason.

One of the great "troubles" for many folk on the spiritual path is "What is my 'svadharma'?" ("own duty"), or "What is my purpose in life? Why am I here? What am I supposed to be doing?"

These two powerful verses answer those questions. If one becomes fully content, totally satisfied and absorbed in the Self, then there is no particular "duty" or "purpose" to be accomplished, nor is there any reason to do, or not do something.

Recalling Ramana Maharshi's earlier quote, echoed by Nisargadatta Maharaj, and the contemporary Adyashanti,

"If you, who have come to this world alone...subside in Self by knowing what is the reality of yourself, know that that is the greatest help which you can render to all the other people in this world."

If one "subsides in Self", you will likely not find yourself "lounging by the pool", but, instead, you will be engaged in all sorts of activities you could not have imagined, as they arise...now, now, now.

IV, 22

यद्रच्छा	लाभ	संतुष्टः	द्वन्द्व	अतिइतः	वि	मत्सरः
yadrcchaa	laabha	santushtaH	dvandva	atiitaH	vi-	matsaraH
by chance	what comes	content	dualities	beyond	without	jealousy

समः	सिद्धौ	असिद्धौ	चा	कर्वा		अपि	न	निबध्यते
samaH	siddhau	asiddhau	ca	krtvaa		api	na	nibadhyate
the same	success	failure	and	performing action		even	not	is bound

Content with what comes by chance, beyond the pairs of opposites, free from envy, the same in success and in failure (equanimous) - (s) he is not bound even while performing actions.

"Yadrccha laabha" is also translated as "with what comes unasked for, or without having prayed for it".

This verse gives a wonderful, compact summary of the attributes of one absorbed in the bliss of the Self. There is contentment no matter what happens unexpectedly and unasked for. There is no preference whether there is happiness or sadness, energy or laziness, hot or cold, etc. There is no jealousy or wishing ill on another, as one resides in the state which could not be improved by adding to or taking away anything.

Similarly, there is no disturbance whether there is apparent success or failure in any endeavor "in the world". Even when one appears, to others, to perform actions, as (s)he is absorbed in the Self and has no sense of being a "doer", (s)he does not feel that it is (s)he that is doing the actions and so, whatever its outcomes, it does not touch him/her.

If what is described in this verse isn't your experience, then there is still some work to be done.

Some express concern that one will behave with great malice when one awakens and becomes absorbed in the Self. There have been no such instances that have ever been recorded, as far as i know. Without self-referential thoughts, desires and fears, there is nothing that would move you in such a direction.

As we will see later, what happens is ultimately not under our control, whether one is "awakened" or not. The difference is that there is no one to be identified with and attached to the outcomes, good or bad, if one is in the awakened state.

IF SOMEONE IS "AWAKENED" WILL THEY STAY IN THE WORLD?

III, 5

न हि	कश्चित्	क्षणं	अपि	जातु	तिष्ठति	अ	कर्म	क्रत्
na hi	kashchit	kshanam	api	jaatu	tishthati	a-	karma	krt
no because	one	for a moment	even	ever	remains	without	work	doing

कार्यते	हि	अवशः	कर्म	सर्वः	प्रकर्ति	जैः	गुणैः
kaaryate	hi	avashaH	karma	sarvaH	prakrti	jaiH	gunaiH
made to	for	are compelled	work	everyone	Nature	born	of gunas

Indeed, no one can ever remain for even a moment without performing actions. Everyone is made to act, helplessly, compelled by the inherent qualities arising from their true Nature.

"Nature" here would contemporaneously incorporate genetics, environment, conditioning, when and where you were born, etc.

As discussed in the previous verse, there is a distinction between those who have transcended the gunas, the "guna-atiitaH" (the "awakened" ones) and the "unawakened" ones based upon whether the self, or the Self, is believed to be acting.

In the guna-atiitaH, one is absorbed in the Self, and although actions continue to manifest as that particular body-mind is

73

impelled by its Nature, there is no self who has the illusion that they are the "doer" of any of those actions. For the unawakened, there is only the self that is evident, who is "made to act, helplessly, by the gunas born of its Nature." Neither has "free will" or "is in control", but in the "Self" case, they realize they don't.

So no matter what happens, I really didn't do anything?

V, 8

नैव	किञ्चित्	करोमि	इति	युक्तः		मन्येत	तत्त्व वित्
naiva	kinchit	karomi-	iti	yuktaH		manyeta	tattva vit
not	anything	do I do	thus	absorbed in Self		would think	Truth knower of

पश्यन्	शर्ण्वन्	स्पर्शन	जिघ्रन्	अश्नन्	गच्छन्	स्वपन्	श्वसन्
pashyan	shrnvan	sprshan	jighran	ashnan	gacchan	svapan	shvasan
seeing	hearing	touching	smelling	eating	moving	sleeping	breathing

"I do nothing at all", thus would one absorbed in Self, the knower of the Self, think –

seeing, hearing, touching, smelling, eating, moving, sleeping, breathing

V, 9

प्रलपन्	विसर्जन	ग्रहन	उन्मिषन्	निमिषन	अपि
pralapan	visrajan	grhnan	unmishan	nimishan	api
speaking	releasing	holding	opening eyes	closing eyes	even

इन्द्रियाणि	इन्द्रियार्तेषु	वर्तन्ते	इति	धारयन्
indriyaani	*indriyaarteshu*	*vartante*	*iti*	*dhaarayan*
sense/action organs	in their objects	are engaged	that	knowing

speaking, letting go, holding on, even opening and closing the eyes – knowing that it is the organs of sense and action engaged in their objects

For the "awakened" one absorbed in the Self, there is the clear realization and understanding that (s)he really does nothing. What may appear to others as willful action is just the organs of action and sensation moving among their objects.

There are many famous verses in Ch. IV, which is actually subtitled- "Knowledge and Renunciation of Actions". For example, Verse 17 - "…The true nature of action is inscrutable", Verse 18 - "He who finds inaction in action and action in inaction, he is the wise one among men; he is engaged in yoga…" and Verse 20 - "Having given up attachment to the results of action, he who is ever-contented, dependent on nothing, he really does not do anything even though engaged in action."

When one really sees that when actions are being performed, there is no role played by the "ego/I" in the performance, these verses become obvious. If you watch the self-referential, "blah, blah" mind while actions are being performed, it is apparent that the narrative has nothing to do with what is really going on - the actions are occurring "all by themselves". The "blah, blah" mind is off somewhere else, talking to itself about something that has nothing to do with "now, now, now".

If you had to mentally, consciously "will" every action into being, you would never move. How would it be possible to command every single action of every muscle, ligament and tendon, every mixing of specific neurochemicals to initiate the motion in the motor cortex, and then synchronize how everything flexed, turned, and twisted? How would you coordinate the supporting muscles, blood, digestion of the food, movement of glucose and oxygen to feed the muscle and then burn it, to generate the energy for the action? How could we possibly believe that *we* did those actions?

The famous experiments of Benjamin Libet in the early 1980s definitively demonstrated that the brain's motor cortex initiates the actions well before the "I" is even made aware of them and well before they are performed. These experiments, controversial at the time, have been validated by many, many researchers with the latest technology. The result is no longer in dispute. These experiments made it abundantly clear that our "willing" every action is an illusion manufactured by the brain.

There were, no doubt, some evolutionary advantages to creating the illusion of "free will", but it is increasingly being regarded as now being "maladaptive" as it creates great confusion, anxiety and unhappiness; our problems are now not "lions, tigers, and bears", but largely self-referential mental creations.

WHO IS RESPONSIBLE FOR GOOD DEEDS AND BAD DEEDS?

V, 10

ब्रह्मणि	आधाय	कर्माणि	सङ्गं	त्यक्त्वा	करोति	यः
Brahmani	*aadhaaya*	*karmaani*	*sangam*	*tyaktvaa*	*karoti*	*yah*
to the Self	by surrendering	actions	attachment	by renouncing	acts	who

लिप्यते	न	सः	पापेन	पद्म	पत्रं	इव	अम्भसा
lipyate	na	saH	paapena	padma	patram	iva	ambhasaa
affected	is not	he	by sin	lotus	leaf	like	by water

(s)he, who does actions, surrendering them to the Self, and giving up all attachment to them, is not affected by sin, just as a lotus leaf is not affected by water.

you are not affected by the outcome of any action, bad or good deed alike if you have let go of any attachment to the action and surrendered it to the Self; it becomes a practice to remove residual attachments impeding absorption in the Self. This becomes apparent in the next verse.

HOW DO I PERFORM ACTIONS WITHOUT BEING ATTACHED TO THE RESULTS?

V, 11

कायेन	मनसा	बुद्ध्या	केवलैः	इन्द्रियैः	अपि
kaayena	manasaa	buddhyaa	kevalaiH	indriyaiH	api
by body	mind	intellect	merely	senses	even

योगिनः	कर्म	कुर्वन्ति	सङ्गं	त्यक्त्वा	आत्म	शुद्धये
yoginaH	karma	kurvanti	sangam	tyaktvaa	aatma	shuddhaye
karma yogis	action	perform	attachment	giving up	their	purification of

Having given up attachment to results and outcomes, karma yogis, (wo)men of action, undertake actions merely through the body, mind, intellect and senses, for their own purification.

If one lets go of the illusion of control, of there being an "I" who is "doing" something, it is apparent that the body, mind, intellect and senses are performing the action, "all by themselves". Actions do not stop because there is no "I" construct/illusion believing it is "doing" them; they "naturally" continue, as they always have.

Watch for the next five minutes at how little the "I" is even cognizant of what actions are being done, let alone having any concept of exactly "how" they are being done.   In reality, as the earlier verse says, "we do nothing at all".

These five verses lead to a simple and beautiful chant that captures it all.

THEN WHAT IS DOING THESE ACTIONS?

IV, 24

ब्रहम	अर्पणम्	ब्रहम	हविः	ब्रह	अग्नौ	ब्रहमणा	हुतं
brahma	arpanaM	brahma	haviH	brahma-	agnau	brahmanaa	hutam
Self	the ladle	Self	the ghee	Self	the fire	by the Self	is poured

ब्रहम	इवे	तेन	गन्तव्यं	ब्रहम	कर्म	समाधिना
brahma	iva	tena	gantavyam	brahma	karma	samaadhinaa
Self	only	by him	shall be reached	Self	goal	who concentrates

Self is the ladle, Self is the melted butter, by the Self is the oblation poured into the fire of the Self.

Self shall only be reached by (s)he who concentrates on the Self as the objective.

This verse captures, in a beautiful poetic metaphor, the essence of the previous five verses. The well-known and much-performed fire ceremony, in which molten butter (ghee) is poured into a fire while appropriate invocations and prayers are offered, is a powerful image for many cultures and is elevated in this verse to the level of a powerful teaching; all of these elements, including the one who performs the ritual (and even the one(s) watching), are the Self. Most cultures have such rituals in which this metaphor also works.

This verse is used as a meal chant by many Hindus. Most cultures have some before-meal chant or prayer which is typically thankful, but few are so strongly focused on identification of every action being done by "God".

This sacrificial offering of one's actions extends even to breathing, as in the famous verse, IV, 29, "Constantly practicing control of the vital forces by stopping the movements of the outgoing and the incoming breaths, some offer as a sacrifice the outgoing breath in the incoming breath; while still others, the incoming breath in the outgoing breath." This verse is often used in discussion of yogic breathing, or pranayama. The still point of that "sacrifice", where the surrendering of one breath cycle into another occurs, is a powerful window into stillness.

There is also the aspect in this verse of what is known as "jnana yajna" - considering the ultimate Knowledge of Reality itself as a sacrificial act. Verse IV, 33, reinforces this idea; "Knowledge considered as a sacrifice is greater than sacrifices requiring materials...all actions in their totality culminate in Knowledge."

This is so because typically yajnas, or rituals/sacrifices, are done to produce specific material outcomes. Since Knowledge is focused on realization, and ultimately requires the surrender and sacrifice of the "I", it is more demanding and "greater" as it is the sacrifice of all attachments.

ARE THERE OTHER TRADITIONAL BEFORE-MEAL CHANTS?

XV, 14

अहं	वैश्वानरः	भूत्वा	प्राणिनां	देहं	आश्रितः
ahaM	vaishvaanarah	bhuutvaa	praaninaaM	deham	aashritaH
I	the digestive fire	having become	of living beings	the bodies	residing in

प्राण	अपान	समा	युक्तः	पचामि	अन्नं	चतुर	विधं
praana	apaana	samaa-	yuktaH	pacaami-	annaM	chatur	vidham
praana	apaana		combining	digest	food	four	kinds of

Having become the digestive fire, Vaisvaanarah, I abide in the bodies of living beings and combining the praana and apaana, digest the four kinds of food.

This verse and the previous one are often said before meals to keep you periodically reminded to pause and recognize that the Self does everything, every action, even the digestion of your food.

The four kinds of food are classically described as those that are eaten by "masticating, swallowing, sucking and licking". As this comprises, conceptually, all foods, it is customarily taken as a protection from any bad, impure or contaminated food. As many people in India are on a poor, low quality diet, this has great meaning for them.

We now move into four verses focused on "free will", "control" and "surrender", key elements of the Bhagavad Gita, which are strategically and importantly placed as the concluding "teaching" verses of the 700 in the Gita.

WHAT IF I DECIDE THAT I'M JUST NOT GOING TO DO SOMETHING?

XVIII, 59

यत्	अहङ्कारं	आश्रित्य	न	योत्स्ये	इति	मन्यसे
yat	ahankaaram	aashritya	na	yotsye	iti	manyase
that	egotism	relying on	not	I will fight	thus	you think

मिथ्या	एषः	व्यवसायः	ते	प्रक्रितः	त्वां	नियोक्ष्यति
mithyaa	eshaH	vyavasaayaH	te	prakrtih	tvaam	niyokshyati
in vain	is	resolve of	yours	your nature	you!	will compel

If, filled with egotism, you think "I will not fight" - this resolve of yours is in vain; your own nature will compel you!

XVIII, 60

स्वभावेजेन	कौन्तेय	निबद्धः	स्वेन	कामना
svabhaavajena	kaunteya	nibaddhah	svena	karmanaa
born of your nature	son of Kunti	bound	by your own	duty/karma

कर्तुं	न	इच्छसि यत्		मोहात्	करिष्यसि	अवशः	अपि	तत्
kartum	na	icchasi	yat	mohaat	karishyasi	avashaH	api	tat
to do	do not	want	which out of	delusion	you will do	helplessly	just	that

Being bound by your own karma, born of your nature, you, helplessly, will verily do exactly what, because of your delusion, you do not want to do.

OK, but I must be in control!

XVIII, 61

ईश्वरः	सर्व	भूतानाम्	हृद	देशे	अर्जुन	तिष्ठति
iishvaraH	sarva	bhuutaanaaM	hrd	deshe	Arjuna	tishthati
Self	of all	beings	heart	region		resides

भ्रामयन्	सर्व	भूतानि	यन्त्र	आरूढानि	मायया
bhraamayan	sarva	bhuutaani	yantra	aaruudhaani	maayayaa
revolving	all	beings	machine	as mounted on	by delusion

The Self resides in the hearts of all beings, causing them all to revolve, by its Illusive power, as if they were mounted on a machine.

"Maayayaa" can be also be translated as "through Maya", "by delusion", or "as if by magic".

This is a powerful verse, and a popular one. The image of all people being powerlessly mounted on a machine and being moved by the illusions of Maya, by the Self which resides in everyone, is a powerful one. What more graphic description of our powerlessness and the power of the Self could there be?

This recalls the important earlier verse, X, 20 – "I am the Self, seated in the hearts of all beings; I am the beginning, the middle and the end of all beings."

If I'm not in control, then how do I attain peace?

XVIII, 62

तं	एव	शरणं	गच्छ	सर्व	भावेन	भारत
tam	*eva*	*sharanam*	*gaccha*	*sarva*	*bhaavena*	*bhaarata*
in Self	alone	refuge	take	whole	being/heart	son of Bharata

तत्	प्रसादात्	परां	शान्तिं	स्थानं	प्राप्स्यसि	शाश्वतं
tat	*prasaadaat*	*paraam*	*shaantim*	*sthaanam*	*praapsyasi*	*shashvatam*
by	grace of Self	supreme	peace	abode	you will attain	eternal

Take refuge in the Self alone with your whole being. Through the grace of the Self, you will attain supreme peace and abide there eternally.

There is much discussed in this work about the power of "letting go", of complete surrender, as the "last step" in awakening. A point comes in virtually all folks' awakening when the practice gets down to letting go of every attachment, every single one.

This does not mean you can get "there" by giving or throwing away every item, person, possession, etc. to which you are attached. That really doesn't release you from that attachment, as you can still retain the image, feeling, or memory of it.

Complete surrender is of the "one" who is attached, the owner, enjoyer, possessor, and experiencer, whether or not the attachment is still around. Only when that "one" is surrendered, with "your whole being", to the Self, do you find that supreme peace that "passeth all understanding", forever.

In my case, even though the "I" had been whittled down to almost nothing through self-inquiry, negations, and affirmations, there was still a small residue remaining. For me, this residue needed to be surrendered to "something concrete"; "I" was not able to surrender "the rest of me" to the vastness of the Self. Something was needed to take it away.

Although i had been strongly anti-guru, anti-devotional, and anti-bhakti, by this time, "I" had developed a strong bhakti relationship to Ramana Maharshi. Ramana took away the residue. Yes, i do know all of the psychological analysis that is possible around that, but it really worked, really...

These verses are followed by the colorful summary verse, "To you has been imparted by Me this knowledge which is more secret than any secret. Pondering over this as a whole, do as you like". Arjuna later responds saying that his illusion has been destroyed and he will follow the teachings.

IF I BECOME ABSORBED IN THE SELF, WILL I NEED THESE TEACHINGS?

II, 46

यावान	अर्थः	उदपाने	सर्वतः	संप्लुत	उदके
yaavaan	arthaH	udapaane	sarvataH	sampluta	udake
whatever	use	in a well	everywhere	flooded	with water

तावान	सर्वेषु	वेदेषु	ब्राह्मणस्य	विजानतः
taavaan	sarveshu	vedeshu	braahmanasya	vijaanataH
to that extent	in all	the texts	for one who knows Self	knows Reality

To one who knows the Self, who knows the reality, all the texts are of as much use as is a well when everywhere is flooded with water.

"Teachings" here refers to more than just the Vedas, but to all teachings, rites, rituals, practices, pilgrimages, etc. If one is absorbed in the Self, there is nothing that could be taken away, or gained, that would make any difference, or any improvement, in that state, no matter what else might be available.

This may sound like the frequent refrain of "There's nothing you have to do to awaken" from many contemporary nondual teachers, often called Neo-Advaitins. This is even taught by some clearly awakened teachers who went through many years of

91

arduous practices. However, we now know from our cognitive neuroscientific research and exhaustive studies on "brain training" and meditation, that it does in fact require about 10,000 hrs to master any skill whether it is surgery, rock climbing, violin, chess, fire fighting, or awakening.

Dialogues on Teachings of the Bhagavad Gita and Nondual Awakening

The importance of the Bhagavad Gita is not in intellectual discourses or philosophical analysis, but in the application of its teaching to the "battlefield" of everyday life. This is one of the great values of the Gita as opposed to many other spiritual texts. It takes place on an actual battlefield and is focused on successful behaviors, attitudes and actions with regard to the issues on the battlefield of everyday life.

To illustrate these teachings in a contemporary fashion, it seemed useful to include some excerpts from blogposts on dialogues about these same issues with folk who were trying to apply the teachings to their lives. Here are some which deal with karma yoga, meditative self-inquiry, bhakti yoga, free will, practice in daily life, contemporary science and all-pervading Consciousness, etc.

Dialogue with Dominic – Approaching Awakening

Dominic (real name) has a 50 hr/wk supervisory job, wife, new baby, and has been working w/"me" on nondual awakening for a year. There are three posts in the following pages that cover our dialogues. The first Dialogue with Dominic describes what he was going through in the weeks leading up to his awakening. The second describes the "state" he achieved and his "practices" to reach that state as he integrated them into his everyday life. The last describes the weeks after, as the awakening experience ripened. This was really "Do It Yourself" (DIY) nonduality.

This is chronologically the first of the three Dialogues with Dominic; it covers the challenges he faced in his daily life in implementing self-inquiry.

Dominic: Emotions really took over recently. Am working overtime with constant inquiry. Reading Ramana. Who am I? Where am I? Why am I? Inquiry about 20% of waking hours. Whenever it comes up...

Gary: *Great that you are being so diligent w/inquiry. That is the way to make "nonduality", stillness and "no thought", or much reduced thought, a reality...*

D: I'm waking up to the dream qualities of life but the mind can't understand it. Hard to accept that nothing ever happens. As soon as it does it is only a memory. Tough pill to swallow when for so long I thought otherwise. The thinking is what does it...

Am stuck between the draw towards ego and the acceptance of truth. I cry often at the realization of grace. How in a moment all is forgiven so simply. I forgive myself at times and i am able to forgive others. No judgment.

i am really ready, Gary. I have no fight left in me. I surrender. I give up. I will do whatever it takes. The truth is not as easy as I figured it to be or actually it is not as simple as my mind made it out to be. The reality is deeper than i could have ever imagined.

Life can seem like a nightmare. I am a manifestation of life, however there is nothing there. I can't be seen, touched, tasted, heard. I look at my hand but i perceive it so it can't be mine. I don't have or own anything. i am getting to the point where i don't want to even speak. Quiet seems right.

I thought, wanted, and expected it to be more than this.

Lost. Does life give you what you need for awakening? Is that the entire point every day, every moment, that the entire world has been put in our faces to snap us out of the dream and awaken?

i never thought i would be e-mailing you and the kindness I have gotten back is amazing and truly a gift. Thank you is all I could say.

G: yes, everything, everything, has been arranged just so we can wake up. Even what is seemingly the most trivial event, or something you just heard walking through a crowd, can be a catalyst "to snap out of the dream and awaken". Everything matters, *and that's why it is all out of our control_ we can't know which "something" will matter enormously.*

D: Thoughts arise, I feel the emotion brought about in the body. Others are becoming much more interesting to me each moment as i let go of myself. It's fun. I can do this. Persistence. This is like peeling an onion. :-)

G: *Great that you are enjoying "peeling the onion". It really is a fascinating, even exciting and enjoyable process of discovery once you get the hang of it and see that it gets better and better the further you go.*
you have seen much; i suspect more understandings will be manifesting as the onion peels itself.

D: Yes, understandings unfold everyday. The "world" is changing as these realizations happen.
This morning i stood in the garage, looked at a "bicycle", really looked. We call it a "bike" because i have been trained and told a bike looks like this, two wheels, pedals, seat, spokes. What is a "bike"? It is nothing at all and also many, many different things.
I am starting to deeply question what i have been taught. I've been told things for many years. These teachings were just what others have been taught or told prior to being passed on to me.
"Truth" is much different than the "world". Truth is simple, easy, and quiet. When realizations occur a voice says "this can't be true", "there is more to life than this", "You will be a failure if you trust in this", "You will lose everything", "You will die if you let go of everything you have been told". I see this. Many layers to my onion as there probably are for many beings.
My last gurus seem to be "my" wife and child. Trouble occurs when i think about letting go of my attachment to them.
Inquiry and a direct method such as the one we practice is the only way for freedom. I see this more and more every day.
Doing the best i can.

G: Yes, my wife and daughters have been my greatest Zen masters. my deep attachment to my daughters held me back from totally surrendering. I was unwilling to expose them to whatever lay "beyond".

i was totally wrong. When i did surrender fully, and when the page soon turned i was a "better" father than ever before. i had no agenda, so i could be totally present for my daughters w/o bias or "storyline", however they were manifesting and wherever life was leading them.

i was more present for "work" as well, and w/o a lot of interference in my mind clouding my understanding, i did better @ whatever i did, so could also provide for them even better than before.

D: Experienced the "no me, no you, no other" - fun and easy. Different than "i" thought it would be. So much love in the moment and feeling of bliss. Overwhelming joy a couple of times today and right now as i type. Acceptance has a feeling of immense overwhelming love. Love of life. Love of the fact that everything is OK.

Each moment feels like there is an immense space between actions, reactions, thoughts. Habits are not seeming like habits anymore. Space between thoughts, and reaction to thoughts.

A thought arises and it's like, "ok, here we go again". I chuckle at the thought, see it for its futility, smile at it, let it dance a little, watch it leave, and on to the next cloud that passes by.

I feel like i'm winning. But then i see that thought.
There is nothing to win or lose. How could there be?

Question. So life was never Dominic's to claim as his? When Dominic's body is gone, awareness is left. Does awareness have a memory? Does awareness remember experiences? Why am I here? How did i get here?, Where did his imagination come from?

G: *Wonderful understandings arising in your work, and your relationship w/your wife. "Work", even highly complex and fast-moving work like yours, goes on more easily, and more fully, w/o all of the problematic, stress-causing, emotionally-based narrative.*

Re your question on "What happens when Dominic's body is gone?"... As Dominic "goes away", day by day, it is no longer a body belonging to someone, it is just a body moving through its dance until that dance is over. It has always been that way, as the body "does itself" perfectly.

There was a mental construct that some folk agreed should be called "Dominic" that seemed like it inhabited and was limited to, and identified w/that physical form.

As "Dominic" is increasingly seen as just an "idea", just a "thought" that is used to string together other thoughts about experiences and emotions, there is just what was there before Dominic arrived, deep stillness and presence, beingness and consciousness. There is never a time when beingness isn't there...it is ALWAYS there, never MIA.

Physics is coming to the consensus that there is an all-pervading energy that has always been there. We don't know what "it" is, but it follows that we, and everything else, are part of that.

D: There are times when things occur that result in inquiry and I don't react verbally, but they cause anxious feelings. My wife says something, I get jealous, the mind responds with a story. I perform inquiry. Thought disappears, but the anxious feeling stays.

Do these feelings disappear with practice because there is no I, me, my to care about them? Do the thoughts eventually stop coming? Is the point to wake up in the dream state of life? Wake up to who I am? Does it even matter if I continue with inquiry? What's the point of waking up? Why does it matter?

So many questions.
Who is asking them ?
Who am I?
I don't know.
The "I don't know" concept is what drives me.
I want to know.

WHO AM I?
I feel like screaming it!
Who am I?
Snap the hell out of it! Wake up. Stop worrying about stupid shit.
What the hell is wrong with you? You're nuts for thinking this
stuff.

This constant dialogue swirls in the head after "crazy" thoughts
arise..."blah blah" crap. Some days I wish there was a magic wand
to turn it off. In all honesty I wish this was easier, Gary.

I feel like giving up and then not giving up. Sometimes life feels
like a really, really sick joke. Most of humanity suffers through self
inflicted pain on a daily basis created by this thing we call ego, or I,
or mind or whatever label we put on it.

Kind of depressing. Kind of sucks. It's the way it is. We go about
our days playing these fake roles. All I can do is trust and it will be
revealed.

Who is having these thoughts? Who am I?

And as usual there is no thing there.

G: *This "process" is ultimately out of your control. The brain is doing it
"all by itself", so all of the angst and protestations are just the I/me/my
creating stories about a process it isn't involved in, doesn't understand,
and can't find a way to stop. The I/me/my is fighting for its "life".*

99

Re "giving up", try it and see if you can.

Just "let go, let go, let go" of these stories as they arise. As jealousy, with its stories and projections, arises, just ask "Is this true? Can i be certain that it is true?, How do i feel when the jealousy is there? Can i let go of it?" Even if you refuse to let go of it, just considering letting go of it will weaken its neural structure. you can let go of it, really, if you want to.

Yes, thoughts can disappear - you've already seen that. Mediated feelings, even w/o thoughts, like jealousy, will disappear w/practice. Just keep inquiring; there is an I/me/my there someplace that is now not even able to make it all the way to a thought.

As you say "And as usual there is no thing there".

D: At the parents' place there's a different energy, more lighthearted. Father-son, mother-son roles don't seem to be playing out. Just the way it is. Little "blah blah" mind activity so far. The genuine relationship feels better.

Direct inquiry has found its place in my heart. Too simple to not do it. Catching thoughts as they occur and performing inquiry is like pouring water on a spark before it turns into a fire.

Questions are often arising about what it is like after the I, me, my thoughts have surrendered? Then I remember to ask. Who is having these thoughts about the future?

Will there be any more questions?
Then it occurs to me.
Most likely not because who would ask them?

Or if there are questions, they are simple, straightforward, and without attachment..."What time is the meeting?", "Where is the wedding? "How old is s(he)? With no I, me, or my, then there is nothing to gain. Nothing to lose. Nothing to be afraid of...on and on...a bunch of no things. The clouds are clearing away and the sun is starting to shine. Slowly but surely.

Thank you as always.

G: The simple questions, like "Where is the meeting?" will continue. That is "semantic" information, not emotional/autobiographical information which is where the problems arise. you can accumulate and process all of the semantic information that your job, family, etc. require w/o getting dragged back into the emotionally-charged, self-referential narrative.

As/if/when you come upon an emotional-engaged thought, or sensation, just use the inquiry. As you said "Catching thoughts as they occur and performing inquiry is like pouring water on a spark before it turns into a fire."

Don't worry...there is nothing there to fear, no crushing pain or horrendous suffering beyond imagination, no inability to function, etc. Just stay present w/the inquiry.

Things are going very well. Old troubled relationships change as the same folk isn't there anymore to hold the old stories.

D: Keeping this short. I now understand why some choose silence as the method of communication. Words and speaking are like the ant in comparison to the universe. So content knowing everything is as planned.

Quantum Theories About Reality

Andy M.   The Scientific American article "The Quantum Theory and Reality", said "The doctrine that the world is made up of objects whose existence is independent of human consciousness turns out to be in conflict with quantum mechanics and with facts established by experiment". Is this statement in conflict with the reality you experience?

G. Hi Andy M. I liked the paper; am familiar with quantum entanglement, Bell's theorem, quantum nonlocality, etc. i liked the conclusion *"Most particles are aggregates of particles that are ordinarily regarded as separate objects that have interacted at some time in the past with other objects. The violation of separability seems to imply that in some sense all these objects constitute an indivisible whole."*

As background, quantum theory and Heisenberg's uncertainty principle tell us that an unobserved small object (electron or a photon/particle of light) exists only in a blurry, unpredictable state, with no well-defined location or motion until it is observed. The not-yet-manifest condition is described by a wave function, a mathematical expression of the probability that a particle will appear in any given place. When an electron suddenly switches from possibility to reality, physicists say its wave function has collapsed.

When two particles are close together they are "entangled", i.e. they have the same wave function, so when we measure one particle, the other particle's wave function collapses immediately. This "entanglement" exists "forever" for those two particles even if they are moved to different ends of the Universe; they are "inseparable".

i have worked w/some quantum cosmologists on understanding how "quantum level" can extend to "macro level" like "everything is One". (See blogpost "Is the universe alive? Does it evolve, think, reproduce?") As to "my" experiences, what "i" see appears "unreal", somehow created by the mind and is just patterns of energy.

Distinctions between what we resolve are only apparent and are defined by the limitations of our perceiving apparatus, i.e. dogs, insects, or your partner, see a different world than you do. This fits with there needing to be an observer to see it, as required in quantum mechanics, even for big things, like "everything". Although some quantum physicists held that quantum physics only applied to very small things, it doesn't "look" that way "mystically" and increasingly "scientifically". This "Bell's Theorem" paper helps with that.

To clarify about "my" mystical experiences, these experiences are not unique to "me". These mystical states are widely cited in mystical/spiritual and psychedelic literature. The posts "which is more pleasurable...psychedelics, the nondual state, or sex", and "Seeing everything as one? What is mystical? What is really "real"? - the science", describe these states, and the great similarity between how they arise neuroanatomically, both nondually and psychedelically.

Returning to quantum mechanics, Bell's Theorem experiments conducted by Nicholas Gisin in 1997 demonstrated that two particles can communicate "instantaneously", at least 10,000 times faster than the speed of light (FTL). For this work, Gisin received the inaugural "Biennial John Steward Bell Prize for Fundamental Issues in Quantum Mechanics and Their

Applications" in 2009. There is no generally accepted model for how this happens; it violates Einstein's theory that nothing can travel FTL. Approaches like the Alcubierre drive, or transferrable wormholes have been conceived, but are highly controversial.

One controversial theory, gaining in popularity, is Amit Goswami's (with whom i had the pleasure of doing a workshop) "self-aware universe". you can see him in "The Quantum Activist" and "What the Bleep Do We Know?" or read his ground-breaking "The Self-Aware Universe; How Consciousness Creates the Material World":

John Hagelin, whom I met at last year's SAND conference in San Francisco, is a world-renowned quantum physicist, educator, public policy expert, and leading proponent of peace. He conducted pioneering research at CERN (the European Center for Particle Physics) and SLAC (the Stanford Linear Accelerator). He has credibility as he has some highly cited work in the physical sciences. An interview with John about his "Unified Field Theory" is on YouTube. Here are some comments that John provided to me that summarize that talk:

JH. What is consciousness? And where does it come from? We are in a position to answer those questions now. Regarding consciousness, there is not yet a consensus in the scientific community, but with the discovery of the unified field, we now understand that life is fundamentally One.

According to modern physics, the foundation of the universe is a single unified field which unites gravity with magnetism, light, radioactivity, and the nuclear force. All the forces of nature and the so-called particles of nature are now understood to be One. They are just different ripples on an ocean of existence—the unified field or superstring field.

This single field of intelligence is the basis of everything—mind and matter, our separate consciousnesses, my consciousness, your consciousness. Everything is nothing but That. We individualize our consciousness through the filter of our nervous system. We create our own realities.

At the basis of life's diversity there is Unity; you and I are One. That Unity is consciousness—Universal Consciousness. Consciousness is not created by the brain; it is fundamental in nature.

We are used to the concept that we are living in a material world, a dead world. Classical physics is billiard-ball physics—the interaction of discreet and separate objects. But in quantum mechanics, that concept is replaced with wave functions. The quantum world is made of waves of information.

And what is the field that is "waving"? A universal ocean of pure potentiality—which is what we're made of. The unified field is pure abstraction—pure abstract Being—pure, abstract, self-aware consciousness, which rises in waves of vibration to give rise to everything we see in the vast universe.

So a wave function is really made of the same stuff thoughts are made of. We are living in a thought universe. The deeper you go, the less inert, the less dead the universe is; the more alive, the more conscious the universe becomes. And the unified field is pure Being, pure consciousness. Intelligence is the fountainhead—dynamic, self-aware intelligence.

All pervasive "dark energy", 73% of the mass/energy of the universe, discussed in earlier blogs, could be this "self aware consciousness". The recent demonstration of the Higgs boson validates the concept of the Higgs field; it is all-pervasive. we have no idea if it, or "dark energy", is "self-conscious". If it is, it makes "telepathic" communication and "synchronicities" in our lives much easier to conceptualize. If IT is everything, IT is communicating w/Itself, is "everywhere" and "everything". It seems impossible to know "ITs" state as it is far more intelligent than we will be able to grasp. Also, since we are IT, we cannot stand "outside" of IT and "understand" IT.

Q. It there anything from the latest scientific discoveries, like the Higgs field and boson, which say anything about how it would be possible for "consciousness" to create matter?

G.   Yes, the recent discoveries do a lot to enhance the understanding of how "consciousness" can create matter.

Serious scientists now postulate that the universe is conscious, "self-aware" and all-pervasive. Could the Higgs field, described by Peter Higgs and its enabling Higgs boson, be this "self-aware all-pervasive consciousness" that the ancient texts described?

The fundamental issue hinges on how quantum physics actually "works". Two fundamental principles are uncertainty and complementarity. These principles demonstrate that there is no reality until that reality is perceived.
This is not just a matter of interpretation, but reality itself is actually changed just by the observation of it.

An example is if a star several light-years from the earth emits a "probability wave" of a potential photon which spreads outward spherically across the universe. When an observer "sees" the probability wave, it collapses and the light from the star is seen. This immediately changes the whole universe as no subsequent observer can see that photon.

In a quantum world, the question arises as to what an "observer" really is. Can your pet, an amoeba, or an electron do it? How do "we" collapse all of the wave functions in all of our electrons, atoms and molecules in ourselves and in "our world"?

Some noted scientists, like Fred Alan Wolf [1]postulate that this "observer" extends all the way down to the firing of individual neurons, in fact all the way down to individual nerve cells. Wolf believes that each atom is "self-reflective", that the atom "notices itself", which creates reality at the atomic/level. This is the first step in the cascade upwards to our observation.

Wolf further postulates that "our mind" is the sum of all of the choices of all of the atomic "minds"; somehow "consciousness" is able to sense and collapse them all on an atomic scale.

As to how this collapsing of the probability equations could be done by "consciousness", we can look at the recent Higgs field/ boson validation. This does appear to demonstrate how matter is created by consciousness, i.e., matter is an "epiphenomenon" of consciousness, rather than the traditional viewpoint that matter somehow creates consciousness.

Wolf, using the widely accepted "Standard Model", describes how the Higgs field interacts with "potential particles" traveling at the speed of light, by visualizing the particles as "funny, half-twisting, half turning light somewhat like when a diver does a spiraling half twist". These particles possess the unique properties of a ½ spin, and of being "left handed". When they encounter the Higgs field, their spin axis is rotated, and they are slowed down into a zig/ zagging motion, which collapses their wave function and makes them manifest as matter, specifically electrons and quarks, the building blocks of the universe.

Other particles, like neutrinos, which do not possess the ½ spin or the left-handedness do not interact with the field and pass through at light speed.

What we do not know, yet, is whether the Higgs field is "conscious" and is "the mind of God", and whether the Higgs boson, which drives this process, really is the "God particle" as some have claimed. If it is "conscious", many folk believe that its consciousness will be far above ours, perhaps so far beyond that we will never be able to understand it, much like 2-dimensional beings trying to grasp 3-dimensional reality. We certainly won't be able to understand it with self-referential thought.

Wolf firmly believes that the field is conscious and intelligent:

"...from the beginning of time--to the end of time, an ultimate intelligence, call it what you will, guides and directs the various activities of everything in the universe in an unfathomable, unseen way."

"...what we call God continues to create, with infinite intelligence, every billionth of a billionth of second. What is created with this perfect intelligence reflects and modifies everything at every instant and at every level."

THE ILLUSION OF FREE WILL AND CONTROL

SK: By both scriptural study and introspection, I got the realization that free will is an illusion. Our thoughts and actions are automated processes without any volition. The only thing that seems to be distinct is my own consciousness (..."I am" and..."I exist"). These rise from within me and manifest without my volition.

Isn't this very process of finding enlightenment a predetermined process? Can I achieve enlightenment or is it more accurate to say that enlightenment happens to me? That the very process of finding enlightenment is subject to the mandates of fate is disconcerting.

G: You have seen the blogpost "You say 'we have no free will', and 'we're not in control'". There is little doubt w/in cognitive neuroscience community that free will, and our ego/I, is an evolutionarily-derived construct, just something that our brains manifested.

It logically and necessarily follows that even "enlightenment" is predetermined. In the blogs and youTube video, "Everything is Predetermined; Einstein and Ramana Maharshi on Free Will", Ramana Maharshi was very clear that *everything* is predetermined, even the smallest things.

On a few occasions Ramana did tell some folk that their only choice was whether to identify either with the screen or the movie. However, that also is not our choice, as you stated; whether we will be able to make that distinction or not is out of our control. Ramana adapted answers to each questioner. Other places he repeated your statement.

That is my lived experience. i was a highly "deterministic" Ph.D. with a lot of success and was certain that i had "done it all myself". When my self-referential thoughts abruptly stopped, i had 1000 folk working for me, four research labs and a budget of $260MM. I found that everything went along perfectly w/no thoughts, no apparent "doer" of anything, or anyone who could manifest. There never was "free will". There was no logical alternative.

The same applies to my "awakening" process. There were many serendipitous twists and turns, spiritual teachers of many types and many insights, different practices, etc. The big shift occurred unexpectedly; not where, when, or how it was expected. What manifested was beyond anything i could have imagined.

SK: Am struggling recently with these questions and it's very reassuring to find someone who can understand. Few of my family and friends understand where I am coming from. This reveals the hold that the illusion of free will has on humanity. Some questions:

Should folks should be "told the truth"...did a realization of your lack of volition lead to a more fulfilling/enriching (i.e. happy life)? A friend attests that although he knows free will is an illusion, he chooses to live in it and finds beauty in the very illusion itself...is that a misguided belief?

Why do I have a visceral aversion to the lack of free will? How did the illusion even develop?

*Is the realization that we do not possess free will analogous to
the realization/enlightenment of Hinduism/Buddhism/Vedanta?
How does the realization fit into the broader frameworks/goals of
Eastern thought?*

*What would you recommend for me to do at this stage? I don't feel
more "peaceful".*

*As Einstein said, a comprehension that you're not in control does
make you take yourself a little less seriously.*

G. Re: "telling folks the truth?", a big surprise was that, unlike
what i expected of living in terror and fear as i recognized i wasn't
in control, life is blissful, easy; it's a dance rather than a war. i
recognized that i wasn't responsible for the world; it was doing
fine just by "itself" w/o my involvement.

At some level we all know that is the truth - we aren't in control.
We realize that we keep failing at "making things happen" as we
wanted, which generates great insecurity and fear. Once we realize
we can't possibly do it, we're "off the hook". Then you relax into
the reality you've been arguing with unsuccessfully.

We develop an aversion to a lack of free will because we like to
believe that we can control things and if we give up our illusion, we
believe we will be at the mercy of things which we can't control.
we're just afraid.
As to why the brain developed this feeling of "free will", probably,
when symbolic logic emerged in response to solving more complex
problems requiring group efforts, and communication with and
assigning different tasks to different folk was critical, it was an
adaptively-useful "motivating" device. These modifications took
place over many thousands of years about 80,000 years ago.

I suspect that the development of "self-referential" narrative, fears and desires, which would have logically occurred over the same time span, would have been adaptively-useful in those environments. However, as we all know, the world is a vastly different place today. Our "threats" are now largely mentally-created and imagined; a different world from 80,000 years ago. It may be time for another adaptive modification.

On whether "no free will" is the same as awakening, as soon as the page turned for "me" it was obvious that there was no free will as there was no one to have it. Once the "I" is seen through, it all just collapses.

As to how "no free will" fits into "Eastern thought", that is a broad topic as Eastern thought is hardly homogeneous. However, supposedly no word exists in Sanskrit, the root-tongue of the romance languages, for "free will".

As to what you should do "now", ask yourself some questions when some event happens that you become engaged with:

Could i have reasonably expected this to happen as it did?

Was it probabilistically likely?

What had to happen to everyone involved to make this come about just as it did?

Can i predict the outcome of this event on everyone involved and everyone they come in contact with?

Did i consciously choose for this to occur as it did?

If you keep these questions active, you will disabuse yourself of the illusions. If you see enough examples in "real life", the brain will let go of the beliefs.

SK. Thank you so much! Responses definitely helped...

I do believe, w/increasing certainty that we are w/o control. This is increasingly accepted by my mind. Is this realization the same as the realization that there is no "I"? Or is the "lack of volition" realization a subset of the greater awakening?

I have faith that my mind can accept my lack of volition as a perfectly reasonable way to exist in the world. Will keep inquiring to coax my brain into accepting the paradigm.

G. A few folk i work with "get" the entire "no free will/no control" almost immediately. Subsequently, they had to be reminded of this, which was no problem. In some cases, this did not correspond with awakening as some still had work to do. Others progressed a great ways w/o even discussing "no free will"; it later became obvious.

IME, if one awakens fully into "no self", it is impossible to assert that "I am in control", and "I have free will", because there is no one to have it or do it. The illusion of "free will" just falls away.

I am introducing it earlier in my work w/folk as it is very useful at deconstructing the "I". Even if folk reject it, it is possible to get most folk to "maybe that's true, at least sometimes". However, even totally rejecting the option does weaken its hold, as at some level, it has been considered as being possible. This begins to weaken the associated neural networks. We know this from the Sedona/Byron Katie work.

The "I" already knows, at some level that it is not in control. It has been struggling mightily to make everything work out as planned, despite countless failures (and successes) that it had no part in, which it recognizes. It knows that control is impossible. The brain ultimately welcomes the new paradigm and life flows freely and easily when the situation is recognized clearly and fully. Being in control was a hopeless task all along.

stillness

Q. You say that "we have no free will", and "we're not in control". That has been debated forever by philosophers and religions. Everyone knows that they have free will and that they make many choices in everyday life. Why do you say we don't have free will? Is this something that you personally experienced, that you can scientifically "prove", or is it just philosophy?

G. That is an important question in this work. It deeply impacts how we feel about past choices and actions, as well as how much stress and anxiety arise as we plan for the future.

Looking at what highly respected scientists and mystics say and experienced, gives us some useful insights from very different perspectives. Nobel Prize winner Albert Einstein, one of the most important physicists of the 20th century, and creator of the "world's most famous equation", said, perhaps surprisingly:

"Everything is determined, the beginning as well as the end, by forces over which we have no control. It is determined for insects as well as for the stars. Human beings, vegetables or cosmic dust, we all dance to a mysterious tune, intoned in the distance by an invisible piper."

"You can will want you want, but you can't will what you will."

Why would Einstein make such statements? Is there science to confirm them or are they just his opinion?

It is useful to look at complexity and chaos theory and how it applies to free will and control. Complex systems theory deals with interactions between parts of a system and how they affect the behavior of the entire system and how it interacts with its environment.

A complex system occurs when interconnected parts have behaviors that affect the whole system in ways that are *not obvious* from the properties of the individual parts. A system with many parts displays "disorganized complexity". This approach has been used to understand ant colonies, economies, financial systems, social structures, climate, nervous systems, cells, energy and telecommunication infrastructures, etc. Most systems of interest to us are complex systems. This approach yields the famous "Butterfly Effect", which is the metaphor of a hurricane in the Atlantic Ocean being caused by a butterfly flapping its wings in France (or wherever).
As tiny and seemly unrelated events can generate huge and unexpected consequences, Hollywood has used this in "time travel" movies and in books. It explains how, if someone traveled back in time and made some seemingly small change, like getting on a different subway or bus, or meeting someone unexpectedly @ Starbucks, human history could change for m(b)illions of folk.

Applied to free will and "control", several useful principles arise from complex systems:

a). All parts of the system affect, and are affected by, many other parts of the system in a complex web of cause and effect and feedback.

b). Completely unpredictable results can emerge even if the original conditions are known in great detail.

c). Complex interacting systems undergoing change (our lives) are unpredictable.

d). With all the interactions and feedback, staggeringly vast amounts of information are required for even a simple decision. A decision a second later would need completely new information as everything had changed.

We have no idea what our actions will produce over time, who they will affect, and in what way. We also have no idea how our current situation came to be as it is, or whose actions will affect us as the web of those interactions is massively complex and unknowable.

Useful science also comes from work in cognitive neuroscience on free will which began w/Benjamin Libet's work. Libet's work clearly demonstrated that the motor cortex initiates an action well before the "I" is even told about it, and in advance of the action being performed. If we aren't even aware when, or what, action is initiated, how can we be "in control" and where is our "free will"?

Libet's work, which received the inaugural "Virtual Nobel Prize in Psychology", not surprisingly caused a firestorm of reactions, and great hostility from many sides, including other scientists. Nonetheless, in the intervening 40 years, w/much more sophisticated technology and measuring equipment and many studies by many folk, his work stands.

A third scientific approach comes from genetics. The Nobel Prize Winner Francis Crick, the molecular biologist and neuroscientist who, with James D. Watson, discovered the structure of DNA, stated that:

"You, your joys and your sorrows, your memories and your ambitions, your sense of personal identity and your free will, are in fact no more than the behavior of a vast assembly of nerve cells and their associated molecules."

Crick and Watson made their huge discovery in 1953; this quote was the conventional wisdom for some time. However, with the emergence of epigenetics, molecular biology, and improved technology, the answer is more complex.

That genetics, depending on how it is defined, is a major element defining "us" is widely-accepted. The question is how much "we" are defined by genetics and epigenetics, or "nature", and how much "we" are defined by family, friends, where and when we were born, what our environment and experiences were, etc. or "nurture". Since none of this is w/in our control, there is still no free will, but the mix of "nature" and "nurture" is complex, interrelated and likely inseparable. A good overview paper is "Genetics and Causation" by Dennis Noble of Oxford in the Philosophical Transactions of the Royal Society.

my principal teacher, Ramana Maharshi, one of the great sages of the 20th century, who was described by The Dalai Lama as "Ramana Maharshi's spiritual wisdom is guiding millions of people", said of free will:

Q. Are only the important events in a man's life, such as his main occupation or profession, predetermined, or are trifling acts also, such as taking a cup of water, or moving from one room to another?

R. Everything is predetermined.

i was highly "deterministic", certain that all that happened to "me" was done by "me". When the page turned and self-referential narrative, desires and fears fell away, that changed. There was no one to have free will, or control, nor had there ever been; free will and "control" just fell away. There was no new insight from philosophy or the science described above, which came later. There was just no alternative.

STOPPING THOUGHTS

Q1. It is impossible to stop thoughts. Is your "no thoughts" a "forced practice"? Can it be maintained w/o effort?

Q2. Thoughts are essential to nearly every function we perform. Thoughts, before and after any (of my) spiritual achievements are still as they were. I can make my inner voice as loud as it could be before; nor have I changed much about the way the system operates.

The notion that one can do engineering or even speak and have it not involve thought is a conceptual (mis)understanding. Intentions fall into the realm of thought. All physical actions are preceded by intentions. The notion that action can occur w/o thought falls into the same camp.

Q3. A retreatant told us that sometimes he had no thoughts for several days. We actually thought it was a bit funny, since this practitioner was animatedly talking about all kinds of things. So we wondered what qualified as "thought" in his view since he was obviously thinking.

G. These comments on "having no thoughts", my principal ongoing inner state for 14 years, are from prominent contemporary teachers. Much of this misunderstanding comes from confusion on what "thoughts" are and when they are useful, and what "no thoughts" means. The strongest resistance i encounter, quite frankly, is from "spiritual" folk who were not able to stop theirs.

Having no thoughts is not a complex or confusing concept in the traditions in which i practiced. Reduction/loss in self-referential narrative is regarded as a key indicator of awakening and whether the source of suffering, fear, craving, etc. has been reduced or eliminated. Some comments:

Ramana Maharshi

"In samadhi there is only the feeling "I am" and no thoughts."
"There is a state when words cease and silence prevails."

Patanjali's Yoga Sutras (I:2)

"Yoga is the stilling of the modifications of the mind."

Nisargadatta Maharaj

"To be free from thoughts is itself meditation."

Bhagavad Gita (VI: 25)

"With the intellect steadfast, and the mind sunk in the Self, allow no thought to arise."

Dogen Zenji

"Be without thoughts...this is the secret of meditation."

Tao Te Ching (Daodejing)

Ch. 16. "Empty your mind of all thoughts. Let your heart be at peace"

Ch. 20. "Stop thinking, and end your problems."

Padrinho Paulo Roberto (Santo Daime - Ayahuasca Shaman)

"It's all about having no thoughts."

The three questioners are understandably involved and invested in their traditions. After much effort, to discover it *is* possible to end suffering simply by deconstructing the "I" and thereby ending self-referential thoughts, fears and desires by a direct, and simple path, is no doubt a shock.

With regard to thought being necessary for speaking, what is your own experience? Watch your speaking carefully...do you prethink everything you say? Is your talking all "thought up" before you say it? Do you "think" to speak? In fact, speaking, self-referential thinking and problem/planning solving use completely different parts of the brain.

The production of language/speaking occurs in Broca's area on the left side of the frontal lobe.

Self-referential "blah/blah", narrative/thought is generated through/in an area known as the default mode network deep in the center of the brain. If you watch carefully, your "blah, blah" is all about, and contains, "I, me, mine", explicitly or implicitly; this drives our stress, fears, craving, etc. This is 99% of most folks' "thoughts" and is what this work focuses on as it is about reducing suffering.

Problem solving, planning, and other "executive" functions are done largely in the prefrontal and frontal areas. These functions project future consequences, weigh "choices" between options, and determine similarities/differences between things/events and what is "socially acceptable."

Complex problem solving and planning does not use the "self-referential, thought-generating, blah, blah" default mode network. It does, however, employ *non*-self-referential thoughts", which are different in "type" and "feel", for framing and receiving the results of complex problem solving. Self-referential, emotionally-invested thought feels "stickier" w/more "hooks" for grabbing related memories and thoughts.

This difference in feeling can be felt if we compare "How do i get to the interstate?" with "How in the *#^%$ do i get to the %$#@ interstate, NOW??!!!". In the former, the "I" is just how almost all human languages are structured. In the latter, the "I" is heavily, emotionally-loaded. The best paper on this is "Attending to the Present: Mindfulness Meditation Reveals Distinct Neural Modes of Self-Reference", by Farb, et al. in SCAN, 2007.

Fortunately, the brain can recognize and sort these, naturally, and can develop a network to monitor and suppress the emotional "thoughts" and allow the planning/problem solving ones to proceed. The brain, no surprise, would rather have stillness, "now, now, now" and order rather than "blah, blah"; give it enough examples, and it will construct the supportive network.

Complex, insightful problem solving is actually done "off line" in primary consciousness. When answers are found, they are sent through the lateral prefrontal cortex (LPFC) back to secondary consciousness which framed the problem. Scientists can actually detect that the problem has been solved w/EEG w/100% accuracy, 6 to 8 seconds before "you" know it by watching the activity in the LPFC.

Excellent papers in PLoS One and the Journal of Cognitive Neuroscience, respectively, demonstrate this: "Deconstructing Insight: EEG Correlates of Insightful Problem Solving" by Simone Sandkuhler and Joydeep Bhattacharya (2008), and "Posterior Beta and Anterior Gamma Oscillations Predict Cognitive Insight" by Bhavin Sheth, Sandkuhler and Bhattacharya (2009).

Watch carefully yourself when an insightful solution has occurred, and see if the "blah, blah" of secondary consciousness actually solved it, or just talked about it, back and forth, and then took credit for it. W/o the interference of "blah, blah", the planning and problem-solving is actually enhanced w/the increased available bandwidth.

For thoughts and actions, watch carefully and see if your "blah, blah" has anything to do w/what action is actually going on, or if it virtually all takes place "automatically". we know from the "free will" neuroscience work that it is initiated by the motor cortex, not by "you". Do you really have any idea how your hand moves? What if you had to think every element of what's required in detail? Would you ever move?

The common experience of rock climbers, martial artists, elite athletes, painters, sculptors, writers, chess players, etc. is that they have no thoughts when they are "in flow" and at their best. It is *critical* that we can stop thoughts and be fully present, and not just when you're rock climbing or sword fighting.

So "no thoughts" means basically no "self-referential, blah, blah" problematic thoughts. Most folk now have something like 55,000 thoughts/day; 100 years ago, we had 5,000. That sounds like something to work on. Watch your sensations arise, see thoughts about them arise and turn them into emotions, add memories, and more stories, and voila, problems.

DIALOGUES WITH DOMINIC – EVERYDAY PRACTICES FOR AWAKENING

This is the second of the three Dialogues with Dominic (real name), who has a 50 hr/wk job, a new baby, 3 yrs of on/off meditation, and has worked w/self-inquiry w/great results. This one deals with the "state" he achieved and his "practice" to reach that state as he integrated it into his everyday life.

Dominic:

Hi Gary,

What a fascinating difference when the small "I" gets out of the way...Two days of very few "I" thoughts. "Who cares?", and "Who am I?" have been the inquiries that resonate with my inner being. "Who cares?" is a great one for me. I can really feel it...felt good all day. Real light-hearted. Smiled, had some fun.

Even dealing with angry customers was not a problem. I actually enjoyed it which is something that has never happened. There was no "I" there to take complaints personal. No "me" to defend. "Work" was so much easier. Communication with co-workers was easier too...the energy in the body and the energy behind no "I" were awesome.

When I talked to people today I looked them directly in the eyes and was absolutely there for them at that moment. I saw those around me for who they really are.. No judgments or condemnation. No concerns, worries, or fear. Just people talking. Very nice to feel this way.

I will try and I will try not to continue inquiry. At this moment the I may be still hiding out around the corner. Funny thing is, this little "I" is suddenly not so important to anyone. In fact, no one is here today to even care. "Who cares?"..."Well, I do of course, and Who am I?" No answer and that is such a nice feeling.

Ideas came into my head the last 2 days. Spoke to my boss about them today and got the "go ahead" to put together a proposal. The ideas would not have occurred with mental "blah, blah" happening.

Having fun with this thing called "life". Not so bad when there is no one to be bothered.

Also, strange things regarding "coincidences" have been happening lately. Almost as if the Universe is attempting to give "proof" that everything truly is one, i.e. had a thought my wife's sister should get a call from us. Turns out she is having issues. Or I will have a thought and then I will read about it moments later on the internet. Not disturbing self-referential thoughts but rather thoughts just floating by. Not minding but just observing this trend lately.

G. It would be useful for folk to have some indication of how much practice you've done and how much you have been doing @ work to reach this point.

D. i have been meditating on-and-off for 3 years; 2 years w/o any teacher or guidance. i would just try different things that i heard about from a friend, internet, and reading different books. During my first 2 years of practice i was not persistent and often times i found meditation boring and experienced little "success". The first 2 years consisted of meditating in my room and controlling the breath while clearing the mind of any thoughts. Not sure if that type of meditation has a name.

i would meditate for about 15 - 30 minutes/day for 3 - 5 days/ week over the course of the first 2 years. In meditation practice, the mind would only be still for 2 - 3 minutes.

During this last year of practice, you and i began communicating. i found self-inquiry to be much more appealing. i didn't realize i could meditate while walking to work, at work, on the train, at home, eating lunch or any other time during the day when i/me/ my thoughts arise.

I always assumed meditation could only be performed while sitting. i do very little sit-down meditation with the exception of before bed and i actually don't sit - I lay down in bed and perform inquiry before sleeping.

Typical day is as follows:

Wake up @ 6 a.m. -- Not much i/me/my until i leave for work.
6:45 a.m. to 7:30 a.m. Walk to the train, ride train to work, walk to work...Perform inquiry when i/me/my occur which is usually the whole way to work.
7:30 a.m. - 5 p.m. working

A typical workday consists of 20% self inquiry, 80% work.

Inquiry during downtime when I am not dealing with customers or helping employees, i.e. 1 minute of inquiry, help a coworker, 3 minutes of inquiry, on the phone with a customer for 20 minutes, go to a meeting, inquiry for 5 minutes while taking a break, review applications for an hour, talk to customers, inquiry for 5 minutes, read emails, inquiry during an email for 2 minutes because thoughts arose, continue reading emails, inquiry for 2 minutes, etc.

Basically anytime thoughts arise I inquire "who am I?"

5pm-5:45 Walk to the train, ride train home, walk home - perform inquiry as thoughts arise.

5:45 - 10pm - Spend time with family. 10 - 20% of time spent in inquiry as needed. Lately things have been flowing well. Inquiry has been running on autopilot but I choose to persist and go deeper until there are no more thoughts.

10 pm Read
11 pm Lay down, perform inquiry.

I have only been this persistent for a month or a little longer. I just made it a point to inquire whenever thoughts arise. Why not?

10 - 20% of waking hours are spent in inquiry.

Bio; 32 years old, married, newborn daughter, supervisor at a small company. Enjoy ice hockey and grilling. 32 years of mental turmoil, always wanting answers, afraid of just about everyone and everything. Strong sense of lack and not being good enough. Things are improving dramatically every moment. Getting stronger in the Self. I feel this now.

Hope this helps some folk.

Happy

Using Devotional Practices for Awakening

Q1. Would immersing myself in my teachers' presence cut through the ego? For instance my gurus are Christ, Ramana Maharshi, Anandamayi Ma, and Yogananda. I sense them as one presence and have a name for their combined souls which is Christ/Ramana.

If I become immersed in Christ/Ramana will this finally cause the ego to become in the background and cause Awareness to recognize itself? I feel safe when I am in this 'state'.

Q2. Gary, am totally absorbed in the energy of Shiva. Am getting totally engrossed in Shiva. He seems to be enveloping me completely. Am still tearing up with the immense love for Shiva :)))))))).

G. Whether "bhakti", or "religious devotion in the form of *active* involvement in worship of the divine" as practiced by Hindus, Christians and others, is a "replacement" for "nondual inquiry" as a path to awakening, is a great question.

As Hinduism is so misunderstood in the West, it is useful to realize that there is both "monotheistic" and "polytheistic" Hinduism. Hinduism is described as "a conglomeration of distinct intellectual and philosophical points of view, rather than a rigid common set of beliefs, formed of diverse traditions and with no single founder." IME, you can find almost anything spiritual, someplace in Hinduism.

For example, if you look at a gopuram, the towers in many Hindu temples, you will see that there are many "gods" at the lower levels, but when one reaches the "top", it is "Oneness" or "The nondual Infinite". Also, "bhakti" is not merely "devotion" which is how it is often translated in the West, but has different manifestations, both dualistic and nondualistic which have different levels of engagement and goals.

As the questioners' comments indicate, this is not just "yeah, the divine stuff is really cool and i'm 'down with it'". It can reach, in its nondual manifestation, to being "absorbed" in nonduality Oneness. The difference between nondualistic "absorption" and mere "devotion" is revealed in the frequently-voiced statement of dualistic bhaktas (those who practice bhakti); "*i don't want to be sugar, i just want to taste sugar*". This resistance to absorption, and attachment to the pleasure of devotion and to the "I"/ego is the place where most stop, short of "union with the essential nature of Reality and divine bliss."

Bhakti is a cornerstone of the Bhagavad Gita, a principal text of advaita Vedanta and Hinduism. As stated in XI, 54. "By unswerving, single-minded devotion is it possible for Me to be known, seen and in reality to be entered into." Bhakti is traditionally treated as diametrically opposed to "jnana" or "knowledge", which is what "meditative inquiry" is all about.

However, while Ramana Maharshi was the quintessential jnani, he was also a nondualistic bhakta. Ramana's bhakti, as he had no folk as a teacher, focused on Arunachala, the mountain revered by many Hindu worshipers of Shiva. Ramana spent his entire adult life on or around Arunachala. The most popular song @ Ramanasramam, Ramana's ashram in south India, is "Arunachala Siva", or "Arunachala is Shiva". It was the song being sung when Ramana "passed" as a single tear arose and he drew his last breath.

Ramana said frequently that bhakti (nondualistic) and jnana are not different as they bring you to the same place. i was an intellectual folk but as my self-inquiry practice deepened and the self began to fall away, what surprisingly emerged was a deep bhakti for Ramana. This turned out to be critical to surrendering what was left of the "I" in the last stages.

i needed someone to take the "I" residue away, like a Valkyrie, and Ramana obliged. As i was so strongly "anti-guru", this was totally unexpected, and i still honestly don't understand it. IME, it was not jnana or bhakti, but both. The controversial contemporary teacher Andrew Cohen has urged all spiritual folk to investigate bhakti as a way to dissolve the ego that can grow during practice.

Regarding mountains as "sacred" is famously manifested for Mt. Kailash in Tibet, a focus of devotional worship for four different religions - Buddhism, Hinduism, Jainism and Bon. Sacred mountains are a part of many religions and are found all over the world. Circumambulation of sacred mountains is a frequent rite and is often practiced for Arunachala and Mt. Kailash.

Anandamayi Ma is a shining example of nondual bhakta, as she was completely absorbed in the "Divine"; she was described by Swami Sivananda as "the most perfect flower the Indian soil has produced". When asked who she was, Anandamayi Ma said that as she had no existence as an "I", she could not say who or what she

was, and therefore she was whatever the questioner thought she was. When asked about her "path", she maintained that "all paths are my path" and "i have no particular path".
She often said "to find yourself is to find God, and to find God is to find yourself".

As far as working with your "bhakti", you already have your iconic figures; feel their energy. As you move toward absorption in that energy, in which you are feeling safe, feel where/what is "holding back". Move to that and just "let go" of it, again and again. Letting go is the key. Allow yourself, all of yourself, to be absorbed into the Divine energy. Bhakti can take you to the same great Stillness as does nondual inquiry, and IME, it can be a critical part of nondual inquiry as well.

Dealing With Anger

Q. Gary...very happy to be in communication with you. The subjects you touch on are very near and dear to a spiritual practitioner's heart. I had some breakthroughs and now I am more relaxed and happy so there is a different practice. I am dealing less with fear and more with anger that arises in daily interactions that don't go my way! And i find it difficult to do self inquiry on anger/irritation. What can I do about anger?

G. Hi. Sounds like your practice is going well.

What to "do" about anger is a great question that i have been fascinated by. When "the page turned" for "me", self-referential thought basically stopped, as did self-referentially-constructed desires and fears and stories about anger. However, i still had bursts of anger. This anger was fast, "primal", possibly protective, but was so fast that i couldn't get "in front of it".

This anger was disturbing, as i had been told by my parents, family, my strict Methodist church, other religions, etc., that anger MUST be avoided. Nonetheless it was there.

In looking at anger, three types of anger are often classified by psychologists:

a). "hasty and sudden" anger - named by Joseph Butler, an 18th century English theologian and philosopher. This anger is immediate and is connected with self-preservation and occurs in many animals when they are tormented or trapped. This is episodic.

b). "deliberated" anger is related to one's psychological interpretation of having been offended, overpowered, wronged, or denied and a tendency to react through retaliation. This type of anger can go on for a long, long time and can end badly. This is episodically-triggered, but gets much more complex with time.

c). "dispositional" anger is related to inherent character traits rather than to instincts or cognition responding to an episode as in a) and b). Irritability and sullenness are characteristics. This is often physiological, genetic and/or neurological.

we are concerned here with a) and b). Interestingly, most modern psychologists view anger as "a primary, natural, and mature emotion experienced by virtually all humans at times, and as something that has functional value for survival."

Well if it is "experienced by virtually all humans at times", what about our major spiritual leaders, do they experience anger?

The Dalai Lama (who said of Ramana Maharshi's teachings, "Ramana Maharshi's spiritual wisdom is guiding millions of people."), arguably the most universally-respected living spiritual leader, has moments of anger:

I am sometimes sad when I hear the personal stories of Tibetan refugees who have been tortured or beaten. Some irritation, some anger comes. But it never lasts long. I always try to think at a deeper level, to find ways to console.

And the Dalai Lama is not alone; the famous Vietnamese Buddhist monk, Thich Nhat Hanh gets angry:

> *"In the beginning you may not understand the nature of your anger, or why it has come to be. But if you know how to embrace it with the energy of mindfulness, it will begin to become clear to you."*

> *"Our attitude is to take care of anger. We don't suppress or hate it, or run away from it. We just breathe gently and cradle our anger in our arms with the utmost tenderness."*

Thich Nhat Hanh has even written a book on the subject, "Anger; Wisdom for Cooling the Flames".

Ramana Maharshi also got angry and gave advice on how to deal with it. My Zen roshis/masters and yoga teachers also got angry, some of them often and demonstrably so.

So it is safe to assume that "everyone" gets angry.

How does anger arise cognitive neuroscientifically?

Anger is the response to a perceived threat, real or imagined. This could be, a) a physical threat to our body, b) a psychological threat to our reputation, integrity or standing in the hierarchy, or c) a physical or psychological threat to another folk that "matters" to us.

There are two main sites in the brain for anger; a) the amygdala, which operates at an instinctual level, and is very old on an evolutionary scale, and b) the neurocortex, which is more recent evolutionarily and is responsible for the intellectual abilities, among other things, of higher primates and some other species. These play different roles in anger and are to some extent interrelated.

When we encounter a threat, the alert goes directly to the amygdala. Because this is a critical element of the survival system, information to and from the amygdala moves very fast, approaching instantaneous.

Studies show that information about auditory or visual threat-related stimuli can reach the amygdala by a fast subcortical (below the cortex) thalamoamygdalic route as well as by a slower thalamocortical- amygdala pathway (Le Doux, J. 2003, in "The Emotional Brain, Fear and the Amygdala" in Cellular and Molecular Biology.).

Luo, et al. in "Emotional Automaticity is a Matter of Timing" in the Journal of Neuroscience in 2010, confirmed these two different amygdala responses and routes - a fast response in 30 to 140 milliseconds, and a later response at 280 to 410 milliseconds which goes to the frontoparietal (neo)cortex for more elaborate processing. The fast response is described as "rapid *preattentive* detection of threat-related stimuli", i.e. the response occurs before we can even "pay attention" to it, in work by Le Doux, Armony, Anderson, and others.

The amygdala sends the signal to our hypothalamus, the brain's hormone control center, which instantly pumps out adrenaline and cortisol to prepare to fight or flee (or freeze on the spot).

So what to do about these two angers; "hasty and sudden" and "deliberated", in our meditation, and in everyday life?

i ultimately accepted "hasty and sudden" anger and focused on what i could do something about, i.e. "deliberated" anger, the processed kind, which rarely occurs for "me" as it is "self-referential". The "hasty and sudden" anger can arise when i am very tired, or my blood sugar is very low - the same situations in which thoughts start for "me". If it arises, the old standbys come in,

"Where am I?", "Whose anger is this?", etc., and keep "deliberated" anger from arising.

The Dalai Lama and Thich Nhat Hanh, consistent with their practices, counsel folk to be present, mindful and aware, and focus on the after affects, and accept, even welcome, the initial spike of anger as a teaching.

It is interesting that in contemporary psychology, there also is little/no focus on suppression, with all of the focus being on "anger management".

What Is Ramana Maharshi's "Direct Path" to Awakening?

Q. Ramana Maharshi described a "Direct Path" to nondual awakening to reach the "thought free" state? What is that? What makes it "Direct"? How does it work?

G. Many traditions regard the "thought-free" state as their goal for nondual awakening, as thoughts cause our stress, anxiety, worry, craving, etc. The name "Direct Path" for the approach of self-inquiry as a route to nondual awakening comes from its most famous modern advocate, Ramana Maharshi:

> *"When the mind unceasingly investigates its own nature, it transpires that there is no such thing as mind. This is the direct path for all".*

This is Ramana's direct approach - there is no religious doctrine, no place to go or lengthy training, nothing except just investigating what your mind is.

This self-inquiry approach was also recommended by Nisargadatta Maharaj, Eckhart Tolle, Adyashanti and earlier folk.

In "my" book, *Happiness Beyond Thought: A Practical Guide to Awakening,* there are approaches/questions that provide insights and understanding of your mind and thoughts which are the core of "The Direct Path":

Why do we even have an "I" with its self-referential narrative "thoughts"? If you were interviewing the "I" for a job, what would its "job description" be?

When i ask folk those questions i get: "protect me from harm", "make good choices", "remember what is important", "remember only good experiences", "don't obsess about the past", "make me happy", "know what's going to happen to me", etc. Is the "I" really capable of delivering on these expectations? Can your thoughts really do that?

What types of thoughts do you have? Have you ever looked at them?

Just take a few minutes and sit quietly, just watching the breath. C'mon just do it; FaceBook can wait...Let the breath slow, and focus on the exhales, until you can see separate thoughts or short thought streams on one subject. Create three buckets for different thoughts. If thoughts were real, you could use external buckets, but since thoughts are just thoughts, you will need internal buckets (also only thoughts.)

The first bucket is for thoughts about the past: pains, pleasures, regrets, joys, "shudas," "cudas," etc. The second bucket is for thoughts about the present: what is NOW, right this instant. The third bucket is for thoughts about the future: plans, fantasies, fears, hoped-for successes, pleasures, etc.

Do not count "sensations" as thoughts. If a sensation is followed by naming, categorization, analysis, a story or something to be done about it, that's not NOW. The sensation is gone and thought is on the scene with a doer going to do something with/about it.

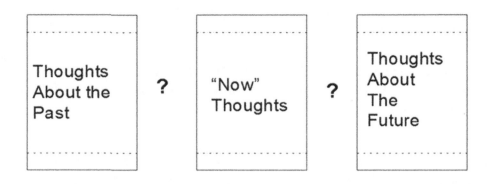

What is the distribution of thoughts between the past, present and future?

For example, you hear a car passing - it can be just the sound without a hearer or something that is heard. If the sound becomes a car, a car outside, a car outside making too much noise, a car outside making too much noise that someone needs to do something about, etc., then that isn't the present, it's the past.

Fill your buckets for a few minutes. Which of your buckets are nearly full? Are any buckets almost empty? What does this tell you?

We live our lives in our thoughts about the past and future, almost never in what is unfolding, NOW. When eating, you think about work. When working, you think about going to a gathering. At the gathering, you think about talking to someone/anyone else, what to say next, what you said that was stupid or brilliant, or being somewhere else. This is a second-hand life. Your thoughts rob you of your life, your happiness and presence. Don't let your life be like the John Lennon quote, "what happens to you while you're making other plans."

How do your thoughts "behave"? Are they about one thing, or many things?

Still and quiet, a piece of paper in front of you, close your eyes and draw the flow of your thought streams. As a thought arises about one topic, draw a straight line until that topic is replaced by a thought stream on another topic. Then draw the line in another direction until that thought stream is interrupted by another. Continue for a few minutes.

What does your paper look like? Is your thinking a long, continuous stream of thoughts about one topic, or is it random, even chaotic, with many short streams on many unrelated topics? Which of the patterns shown was yours?

As many times as I have done this w/folk, no one ever draws a straight line. we believe our thoughts are a series of rational considerations with reasoned conclusions. Is that what _your_ thoughts are? Do you control your thinking? Do you decide what the next topic of thoughts is and when it starts? Who's driving this bus?

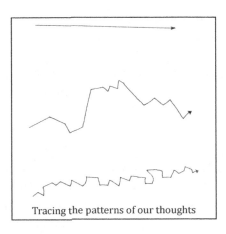

Tracing the patterns of our thoughts

How are our thoughts constructed? What are they "about"?

Again, sitting still and following your breath, focus on exhales until you reach a calm, centered space.

Construct two "thought" buckets. The first bucket is for thoughts with "I," "me," or "my," which can be explicit or implied. The second bucket is for thoughts that do not have an "I," "me," or "my" in them.

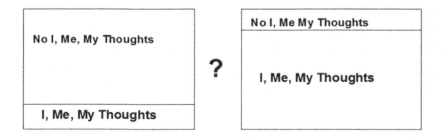

Do Most Thoughts Contain An I, Me or Mine?

After several minutes, examine your buckets. Did you have many thoughts that didn't have an "I" or its sisters somewhere in them?

Most folk find that most of their thoughts contain the "I". It really is *"all about you"*. we believe that our thoughts are about the world's problems, the cure for cancer, etc., when it is actually 99% about us.

This provides an important approach to awakening by using "self-inquiry" into the nature of the "I" as the most *direct* way to be free from the tyranny of narrative thoughts. we can either focus on the myriad objects, an endless process, or we can simply deconstruct the subject. This is the often overlooked key.

There are other useful, powerful exercises you can do:

    a). Where do your thoughts come from and where do they go to?

    b). Can you predict your thoughts for the next two minutes?

    c). Is there only one "I"?

So now what do we do?

Self-inquiry is simply the direct questioning of the nature of the "I", which we have seen is the root of self-referential narrative. Ramana, in his early 20s, gave responses to questions which became "Who Am I?", one of the most succinct and direct discussions on how this work is to be done. It is a short, free, downloadable pamphlet. IME, it is all you need. i give it to folk I work w/ directly after a few meetings.

A typical passage, which is a good summary of self-inquiry:

> *"When other thoughts arise, one should not pursue them, but should inquire: 'To whom do they arise?' It does not matter how many thoughts arise. As each thought arises, one should inquire with diligence, 'To whom has this thought arisen?' The answer that would emerge would be 'to me'. Thereupon if one inquires 'Who am I?' the mind will go back to its source and the thought that arose will become quiescent. With repeated practice in this manner, the mind will develop the skill to stay in its source."*

BTW, Ramana's philosophy is similar to Advaita Vedanta, so similar that Ramana's *Upadesa Saram* or "essence of the teaching" is taught at major Advaita Vedanta workshops and seminars as a complete "short course" in Advaita. However, practices are typically different. For example, some advaita teachers don't condone meditation per se, believing that "as the problem is ignorance, it can only be solved by knowledge, not practices". That certainly hasn't been my experience.

SIN AND KARMA

Q. I'm pretty much sure about predeterminism being true, but predeterminism implies time. For one thing to cause another, there must be a "past". If someone is enlightened, and he resides in "the eternal now", he somehow escapes causality, am I right? Kant had the idea, that "time" and "causality" are in reality just some of the frames that we put our experiences in.

Can this be somehow connected to the notion of karma, and/or freeing oneself from the "birth-rebirth" cycle? It would be great if you could cover the concept of karma and reincarnation; it seems that there are lots of misconceptions.

G. Many of us *believe* in "sin" and "karma" and that our actions are either "good" or "bad" and are recorded somewhere for future judgment when we will be rewarded or punished. This model has existed in many cultures of our interesting species for a long time. IMHO, there are problems with this model.

Who keeps track of what you, and 7,000,000,000 others now and many more before, did in their lives, and how all of it impacted all others? Who decides exactly how "good" or "bad" it was and what it will take to erase it? This gets complicated when one sect or religion believes an act was terrible, while another believes it was "awesome", like flying planes into the World Trade Center.

If each religion has its own judgment process, what happens if someone changes religions, doesn't practice, or never had one? What happens when your religion changes as leaders and cultures change? What matters, what you believe or what your great-grandparents did?

There is also the problem of assigning "responsibility". It would only seem "fair" to be punished if you knew everything that would happen to anyone/everyone who was impacted, forever, when you did something. However, we have no way of knowing, none, what those many, many effects ultimately will be.

Recall the most important decision in your life. Just do it for a few seconds....C'mon...

OK, when you made that decision, did you know a few months earlier that you would have that decision or those options? And, once you (apparently) made the decision, did you have any idea that all that subsequently happened would happen? Was the decision "good" or "bad"?

Select a "big" action of yours, one that stands out. Did it produce only "good" or "bad" outcomes, or were there different sorts of results, with mixed "badness" or "goodness"? Look at a simple "event tree" model of three folk trying to meet for lunch in a week; each of them had many events and choices in the intervening week. If each had only two different outcomes, this is what it looks like - any other branch taken cancels the lunch meeting.

Just imagine how many branches, choices and actions our lives have. Now imagine that with 7,000,000,000 folk, interacting continuously, 7/24. Is there any meaningful concept of the "goodness" of all outcomes?

Consider chess, which is much simpler than our lives with only two families which are fighting, with parents, three pairs of twins and eight younger kids. Guess how many possible sequences of interactions there are...1 followed by 123 zeroes! The number of particles in the known universe is 1 followed by 70 zeroes. How could all of the potential interactions and their consequences in our globally-interconnected lives, ever be judged, or predicted beforehand?

In this context, what can sin and karma mean?

In my experience, as the "I" is realized as an ad-hoc, haphazardly-assembled construct, and begins to dissemble, there is increasingly no "doer", no one to be "responsible" for either good or bad deeds. When the "I" diminishes to where it is only an occasional "visitor" with little/nothing to say, "sin" and "karma" have no meaning.

Regarding the loss of a sense of "personal time", and living "now", they naturally manifest as the "I/doer" falls away. As you cited from Kant, "time" and "causality" are in reality just some of the frames, or mental constructs, like the "I", into which we put our experiences.

Letting go of "sin" and "karma" does not lead to "wild and crazy" behavior. What does result is less guilt, conflict, hypocrisy, dishonesty, and craving as the self-referential thoughts and memories that energize them have fallen away. We cling to sin and karma out of fear that something terrible will happen if we don't have them.

For most folk, they are a great impediment to stillness and happiness. Those who are truly dangerous to society are not moved by "sin" or "karma". This is not an argument for having no laws; i lived in a country w/basically no civil laws but a repressive police state. There was no apparent crime, but the punishments were severe, seemingly arbitrary and w/o trial or appeal. There were also no freedoms or protection for those who could not protect themselves.

Try to imagine what your life would be like without "sin" or "karma". Perhaps, you would find that a different attitude manifests - one of good will and deep regard for "others", because they are now longer "the others", they are really "the One", and you are too.

Letting Go of the "I" and Its Stories

Q. How do I surrender the never-ending stories from my past? The things that others have said to/about me, or events that happened to me seem to continue to affect my life. How can I ever get rid of them?

G. An "I" is assembled around its original elements of genetics and epigenetics, and its environment/experiences, i.e. where and when it was born and in what family, etc. Myriad different-colored "Post-It" notes with all sorts of beliefs, messages, experiences, etc., fly around the "I" but nothing much "sticks" when we are a year old. We are just doing, being, eating, "excreting", crawling, etc. w/o story lines.

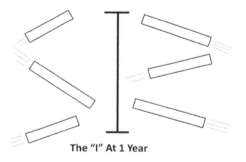

The "I" At 1 Year

Later, these ad-hoc "Post-It" notes begin to stick as Mom, Dad, Grandma, siblings, friends, etc. relate to us and as experiences manifest in our environment. Out of the blizzard of millions of

The "I" At 8 Years

messages, experiences and stories, gathered on different subjects at different times by different brain regions, a few are seemingly randomly and haphazardly selected to "stick" and modify the "I". By the time we are 8 years old, a new "I" has formed.

As we go through our childhood and into our teens, the stories get more complex, interrelated, and who we are gets significantly modified and embellished. Again, out of the millions of experiences and messages that happen, only a few ad-hoc "Post-It" notes are somehow selected to stick and make a new "I". It is composed of many different stories from different times and events that are unrelated, but we somehow try to hold them together in a single "I" story.

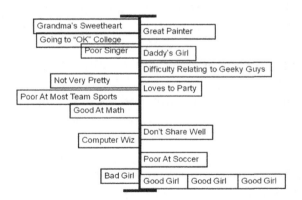

The "I" At 18 Years

In our twenties, with work, increasingly complex relationships, new activities, etc., the "I" gets stuck with more, unrelated, different stories and messages. New ad-hoc "Post-Its" are stuck alongside old existing ones already haphazardly selected. Old stories are kept, and attempts are made to integrate this jumble, as

147

if what Grandma said about us at 4, how poor we were at soccer at 7, or how we looked at 8, means anything today.

The "I" At 28 Years

The critical errors are believing, a) that these stories are related, b) that there is some "reason" they are included other than that they caught our attention or produced an emotion, and c) that they must be maintained even if they may not be true, or if they no longer serve any purpose. As we watch our thoughts, we can see this default program of beliefs running, often destructively.

There are simple, and useful, approaches to seeing if these beliefs are true, helpful and useful and then letting go of them if they no longer serve us.

The best known of these approaches is *The Work* by Byron Katie. She has many books (*Loving What Is*), a website crammed w/ videos, apps (yes, an app), events, schools, 116 YouTube videos, etc.. It all boils down to four simple questions, openly shared on her website, asked around our beliefs and stories:

1. Is it true?

2. Can you absolutely know that it›s true?

3. How do you react, what happens, when you believe that thought?

4. Who would you be without the thought?

You then "turnaround" the belief to its exact opposite, and see if that is as likely to be true as the original belief.

An example would be "XXXX doesn't like me?". Try it and see how it works.

Watch your thoughts and if you see a belief, a story, or a persistent thought stream, make it into a simple sentence. Run through these four questions and turnaround. Watch Byron Katie in the videos; this is a powerful and quick process.

If you practice this, it becomes automatic, running, "in the background", virtually constantly. Beliefs and stories are discarded quickly, almost without being conscious of the process. This is called a "heuristic", a "rule" for dealing for a type of situation, which the brain develops if possible because it is quick and efficient.

As i used this process myself and worked w/folk w/it, it didn't feel "complete". A good "adjunct" process to use with Byron Katie's process is the Sedona Method created in 1952 by Lester Levenson, a physician sent home by his doctors to die. In this dire state, Lester realized two great truths:

1. His own feelings were the cause of all his problems, not the world or the people in it as he had previously thought.

2. He had the ability to let go of those feelings.

Lester's "releasing method" that became the Sedona method is also simple:

1). Allow yourself to feel what you're feeling in this moment

2). Could you let it go?

3). Would you let it go?

4). When?

5). Repeat until you feel lighter, freer, happier, etc.

IME, put these simple questions after Byron Katie's, and the work is more compete. Byron Katie brings you into the feeling, now use Levenson's approach to let go of it.
You may find that with both processes, there are layers "underneath" that may be more fundamental, and more potent. Handle these the same way.

This work has neuroscientific implications, fortunately, for unwinding neural networks associated with specific thoughts or beliefs. Hebbian theory explains how the chemistry of brain synapses works to create networks responsible for beliefs/stories. The more the synapses in a given network are used, and fired, the more they are chemically altered to strengthen the network and increase "synaptic efficacy". As each neuron can have thousands of synapses, the network can be massively complex and tightly wired together.

IME, as networks fire and reproduce a thought, memory, or story, if there is no one attached and willing to take delivery on the "thought", it begins to let go. The next time, it will be less potent, and potentially will disappear. Highly emotional memories w/a large, strongly-connected network may take several Katie/Levenson cycles to "eliminate", but it appears as if each reemergence is less intense and problematic.

These are simple and effective understandings and processes for surrendering the "I", and letting go of suffering. Just do it.

Dialogues with Dominic – Continued Awakening

This is the last of the three Dialogues with Dominic (real name), who has a 50 hr/wk job, a new baby, 3 yrs of on/off meditation, and has worked w/self-inquiry w/great results. This one covers the period after he reached his "state".

Dominic. Any thoughts on dreaming and "blah blah" stuff popping up in the dream state? Felt helpless as inquiry could not assist during sleep. Angry for a minute - caught off guard. Have you experienced something like this? There is some stickiness to the dream. Discouraging.

Maybe life's telling me to press on or encouraging me to face the biggest thing I have to let go of..."my" wife. Not "let go" in the literal sense; I'm sure you know what I mean :).

G. Re dreams, they haven't been useful or important for me. Most cognitive neuroscientists pay little attention to them as they are the brain's nightly housecleaning of old stories, as well as recent stuff going to long term storage or the trash.

Different stuff gets thrown together, just like when memories are recalled and are changed by the addition of something related/

similar but from some other incident. That is why dreams have unusual combinations; they were in the same garbage bag. If memories aren't being used and aren't wanted, the brain throws them out as it "repurposes" valuable real estate.

Whatever your remaining attachments are, the more you let go of them, the more you will be able to deal effectively and openly w/ folk. As you see "others" more clearly and understand things about their behaviors that drove you "crazy" before, it strengthens the relationship. i've been married a long time; been there.

D: Certain things cause discomfort; even w/inquiry there is much anxiety. How can child molestation, rape, Hitler, Jeffrey Dahmer, etc. be acceptable?

Really testing the practice of inquiry; like things are getting "tougher".
Feels like a push to the last bit of surrendering; ego wants to hang on by telling me stories about how "weak" I will be if I give in.

My buttons are really getting pushed. The "I" is using every single trick to prevent progression.

Funny thing is, Gary, w/all this drama, I still know the answer.
I am. That's it. It is enough.

Impressed by your honesty during bloggingheadstv video about loving others as much as "your" children. To truly love another is only loving your Self. I am experiencing this.

G. "Awakening" isn't a destination, it's a continuing process. The Universe keeps "the dance" interesting w/increasingly difficult challenges as one "progresses". you will never get a challenge you can't handle, but it may stretch you to your limits. As Harada Roshi says "Enlightenment is capable of endless enlargement".

As you keep clearing out the rocks and weeds, the lake keeps receding and more rocks, some long buried, become visible and they too will be cleared away. Many folk trod this path before...not all were successful, but some were. It is all about persistence and courage.

Speculation about Daumer, Hitler, etc. is the activity of the I/ego trying to find something, anything to hinder progress; it is endless and fruitless.
Progress from where you are is inevitable, no matter how much the "I" whines and tries to find distractions. The "brain" will not go "back", as you have discovered.

D: I am truly scared...the ego is testing me to the extreme.
Whenever I recognized a decision was "ego based", it resulted in fear with a capital "F".
Those closest to us bring us to the heart.
Crying.
I now get there is nothing to get. I thought there was something to get, to realize. But this is it. No more, no less. Why didn't you tell me? Smiling.

G. i knew you would come upon it at the perfect time, and you did... Telling somebody ahead of time is not useful as folk get sidetracked and believe they are "done" when they aren't.

D. It's fun being aware of "others". my wife is going on and on about this and that... I look at her with a smile, seeing her for who she really is and nodding at the beauty. This is a gift.

And all i can say is thank you. Grace is so deep.
When it touches you, it hits home; the real home.
She certainly has been a super guru. :-)

D. One of my favs:

"Self-inquiry is the one, infallible means, the only direct one, to
realize the unconditioned, absolute Being that you are." Ramana
Maharshi
Enough said.

G. Yes, "enough said".

D....1 + 1 = 2. The problem with that logic is that nothing is just
"one". 1 coffee cup has many different components, yet we call it
"1". Nothing of this world is "1 thing". Nothing and everything is
more accurate.

Smiling

Just being aware is enough. Shifts occur as this is realized, lived,
felt. Hearing sounds for the first time. I was unaware of the energy
and life occurring around me, because "I" got in the way.

Happy, sad, scared, afraid, worried, angry, on and on...just labels
for emotions...no more, no less and increasingly less bothersome.
Everything is well. How could it not be. Still smiling.

Someone says "i did this to you", or "you did this to me", but no
one does anything to anyone. The truth is quite different. As
soon as something is "done", it is gone. Nothing that is "done" can
penetrate the Truth of who we are. Amazing.

154

Grace in every instant, moment after moment. How calming is that? Peaceful to know it wasn't my choice. It just goes on and on. I am not going anywhere ever, am i, gary?
Smiling a lot today!

G. Yes, if you are "now, now, now" and surrender into the understanding that you are not in control, there is no free will, and "no doer", it all just falls away. No one ever did anything to anyone. All "doers" are illusions; we are just empty boats bumping into empty boats.

D. Were you pointing me to it until i realized it? There is nothing to realize. Just life. That's it. How nice is that?

G. It is the Universe pointing @ Herself, until She let go of the illusion called "Dominic" and "you" become absorbed in Her. It is all Her dance and She changes it as She changes it.

D. There was never an "i" to begin with so how could i ever go anywhere? How cool is that. Ultimate smiles tonight!! :-)
Really having fun now. . Stillness.

Everything dissolves w/no one to take claim or credit; every idea, thought, opinion, feeling, sensation, worry, concern. It all disappears. Heard it before but experiencing it now; an expanding space between wants and desires. Attachment still present at times but dissolving.

What is left is this emptiness with a beauty that cannot be expressed. It is love to its fullest extent. This realization makes me cry; overwhelmingly, perfect. What was misery is actually perfection. What will be left when there is no body? If the Self never goes anywhere where is the Self? Where am i?

Deep in this stuff. Losing my grip a little bit. Why has it taken so long to be real with someone?
Funny how she dances...

Work experience seems to be improving dramatically. Every day, amazement happens. Nonresistance to what occurs creates extreme enjoyment in simple tasks. Sit back, relax, and enjoy the show. So very shocked that functioning happens. Watch workplace egos collide.

Every day is an awesome adventure; so grateful.
Going beyond thinking is amazing.
We don't know anything; in that beauty lies.

G...you are seeing the process in its perfection unfolding "all by itself".

D. Things become more aligned when we act naturally. As you said, there is just this, and this, and this. Realizing there is nothing to realize is the gift of life, freedom, serenity.

The most amazing part is that there are no mistakes, no sins, no pain, no lust, no hate. Truth is heaven in every moment. All was lost and now it is found. Grace. How sweet it is. Really.

If there is divergence from Truth, there is divergence from life, the universe, etc.

Always cool emailing with you.

G. Folk miss the enormous "upside" of just living in the "now", in the "just this, and this and this". Once it is fully experienced and lived in, one wonders how they ever found it acceptable to live the way they did before.

156

*It is **that** good and it is possible right here, right now. We just have to get out of the way and recognize that "we" are not now, nor ever were, in control and that whatever happens is "perfect" just as it is.*

D. Having so much fun with life now. Still clinging every now and then. Still surrendering, but there is just this and this and this. . . Letting thoughts rule is insane.

Struggle with wanting to help my wife "see". And, then, "who am I?" Then it goes away, just as it occurred.
So very happy.

G. One sees others suffering, and wants to relieve it, but that too, is out of our control. The clearer and more present one is, the more possible for some deep understanding to unfold in unexpected and amazing ways.
*The great lesson from those close to us is to see where **we** are still attached, where **we** are holding on. As i let go of attachment to an outcome, then the Truth emerged in holistic and healing ways. The answer is always the same, "let go, let go, let go".*

D. These good feelings continue; nice things continue to occur. What was considered "bad" or "wrong" is no longer.

Not so hard with a little dedication and persistence. Often times that word "persistence" was used when guiding the path; absolutely essential.
Starting to really feel the Self. Disorientation is happening lately w/the dissolution of time.

Letting go of the body has been a trip.

Went to work today as the "backseat driver" which occurs more often. Spent an entire day not having many thoughts. No one noticed or cared.
An 8 hour day without thoughts happens without strain.

Thank you for pointing me in the direction.

I have no more questions. I also have no answers. Time to just be me.
Living life now. Saved as some would say... Reborn... Or died...who knows...
I don't know anything, and what I do know can't be described.
Thank you.
Dominic

BIBLIOGRAPHY

Aruna, A. K., *The Aruna Sanskrit Language Course: Unlock the Bhagavad Gita in Its Sacred Tongue,* Bakhaka Mountain Media, Saylorsburg, PA (2008).

Balsekar, Ramesh S., *The Bhagavad Gita; A Selection*, Zen Publications, Mumbai, India (1995).

Dayananda Saraswati, Swami, *Bhagavad Giitaa: Home Study Program*, Arsha Vidya Gurukulam, Saylorsburg, PA (1989).

Dayananda Saraswati, Swami, *Talks on Vivekacuudaamani (One Hundred and Eight Selected Verses)*, Swami Sri Gangadharesvar Trust, Rishikesh, India, 1997.

Dwoskin, Hale, *The Sedona Method,* Sedona Press, Sedona, AZ, (2009).

Ericsson, K. Anders, et al., *The Making of an Expert*, Harvard Business Review, (2007).

Farb, Norman, et al., *"Attending to the Present: Mindfulness Meditation Reveals Two Distinct Neural Modes of Self-Reference"*, SCAN, 2, 313-322, (2007).

Gambhiiraananda, Swami, *BhagavadGiiTaa, With the Commentary of Sankaraacaarya*, Advaita Ashrama, Calcutta, India (2003).

Godman, David, *Living by the Words of Bhagavan*, Sri Annamalai Swami Ashram Trust, Tiruvannamalai, India (1994).

Hagelin, John, "John Hagelin on Consciousness and Superstring Unified Field Theory", Personal Communication, March 19, 2013.

Houston, Vyaas, *Learning Sanskrit from the Bhagavad Gita*, American Sanskrit Institute, Brick, NJ (2006).

Kapleau, Philip Roshi, *The Three Pillars of Zen*, Anchor Books, Garden City, NY, (1980).

Katie, Byron, *Loving What Is: Four Questions That Can Change Your Life*, Three Rivers Press, New York, NY (2002)

Lao-Tzu, *Tao Te Ching*, Stephen Mitchell, Translator, Harper and Row, NY, NY, 1988.

Nisargadatta Maharaj, Sri, *I Am That: Talks with Sri Nisargadatta Maharaj*, Maurice Frydman, Translator, Acorn Press, Durham, NC, (1973).

Ramana Maharshi, *Talks With Ramana Maharshi: On Realizing Abiding Peace and Happiness*, Inner Directions Publishing, Carlsbad, CA, (2000).

Ramana Maharshi, *The Essential Teachings of Ramana Maharshi: A Visual Journey*, Inner Directions, Carlsbad, CA, (2001).

Ramana Maharshi, Sri Bhagavan, *The Song Celestial (Verses from the Bhagavad Gita)*, Sri Ramanasramam, Tiruvannamalai, S. India, (1995)

Ramana Maharshi, *Who Am I?: The Teachings of Bhagavan Sri Ramana Maharshi*, Sri Ramanasramam, Tiruvannamalai, India, (2004).

Sandkuhler, Simone and Bhattacharya, Joydeep, *"Deconstructing Insight: EEG Correlates of Insightful Problem Solving"*, Journal of Cognitive Neuroscience, PloS One (2008).

Sheth, Bhavin, Sandkuhler, Simone and Bhattacharya, Joydeep, *"Posterior Beta and Anterior Gamma Oscillations Predict Cognitive Insight"* by Journal of Cognitive Neuroscience, Jul; 21 (7):1269-79 (2009).

Sivananda, Swami, *The Bhagavad Gita: Text, Word-to-Word Meaning, Translation and Commentary*, The Divine Life Society, Tehri-Garhwal, India (1995).

Venkatesananda, Swami, *Enlightened Living: A New Interpretative Translation of the Yoga Sutras of Maharshi Patanjali*, Anahata Press, Sebastapol, CA, (1975).

Weber, Gary, Blogposts at   www.happinessbeyondthought.blogspot.com, (2012 – 2013):
    "Does It Take 10,000 hrs to Awaken? NO."
    "Is the Universe alive? Does it evolve, think, reproduce?"
    "Which is more pleasurable...psychedelics, the nondual state or sex?",
    "What is mystical? What is really real? The Science"
    "You Say We Have 'No Free Will' and Are 'Not In Control'"

Weber, Gary, *Happiness Beyond Thought: A Practical Guide to Awakening*, iUniverse, Lincoln, NB, (2007).

Wolf, Fred Alan, *Time Loops and Space Twists: How God Created the Universe*, Hierophant Publishing, San Antonio, TX, (2010).

Made in the USA
Coppell, TX
30 June 2024

34105190R00098